Leadership has evolved. Have you?

THE
MOSAIC WAY

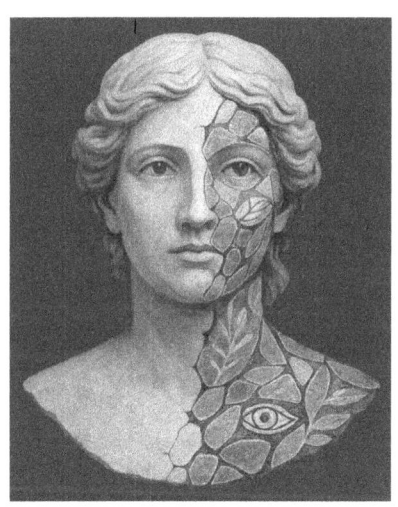

EVOLVE YOUR EMOTIONAL INTELLIGENCE
FOR INCLUSIVE LEADERSHIP *in*
A CHANGING WORLD

Dr. KARISSA THOMAS

© 2025 Dr. Karissa Thomas. All rights reserved.

No part of this publication may be reproduced, stored in a retrieval system, or transmitted in any form or by any means—electronic, mechanical, photocopying, recording, or otherwise—without prior written permission from the author, except in the case of brief quotations used in reviews or scholarly analysis.

The Mosaic Way™ and Mosaic Intelligence Method™ are trademarks of Dr. Karissa Thomas. Unauthorized use of these terms or associated concepts is prohibited. All other names, logos, and identifying marks are the intellectual property of their respective owners.

This book and its accompanying materials are intended for educational and inspirational purposes only. They do not constitute professional psychological, medical, or legal advice.

Printed in the United States of America.

Library of Congress Control Number: 2025909274

ISBN 978-0-9852422-5-1

The unauthorized uploading, scanning, or distribution of this book via the Internet or any other means is strictly prohibited and may result in legal action. Please purchase only authorized editions and refrain from participating in or encouraging the electronic piracy of copyrighted materials.

For more information, please visit:
www.mosaicintelligencepublishing.com
Email: info@mosaicintelligencepublishing.com
Publisher: Mosaic Intelligence Publishing

If—
By Rudyard Kipling (1895)

If you can keep your head when all about you
Are losing theirs and blaming it on you,
If you can trust yourself when all men doubt you,
But make allowance for their doubting too;

If you can wait and not be tired by waiting,
Or being lied about, don't deal in lies,
Or being hated, don't give way to hating,
And yet don't look too good, nor talk too wise:

If you can dream—and not make dreams your master;
If you can think—and not make thoughts your aim;
If you can meet with Triumph and Disaster
And treat those two impostors just the same;

If you can bear to hear the truth you've spoken
Twisted by knaves to make a trap for fools,
Or watch the things you gave your life to, broken,
And stoop and build 'em up with worn-out tools:

If you can make one heap of all your winnings
And risk it on one turn of pitch-and-toss,
And lose, and start again at your beginnings
And never breathe a word about your loss;

If you can force your heart and nerve and sinew
To serve your turn long after they are gone,
And so hold on when there is nothing in you
Except the Will which says to them: "Hold on!"

If you can talk with crowds and keep your virtue,
Or walk with Kings—nor lose the common touch,
If neither foes nor loving friends can hurt you,
If all men count with you, but none too much;

If you can fill the unforgiving minute
With sixty seconds' worth of distance run,
Yours is the Earth and everything that's in it,
And—which is more—you'll be a Man, my son!

TABLE OF CONTENTS

Opening Author's Note ix

Foreword by Martin Scott xi

Introduction
Reclaiming Human Connection in a Disrupted World xv

Part I — The Emotional Landscape of Our Time 1

How a rapidly shifting world shapes our emotional lives—and why emotional fluency is essential for clarity, presence, and resilience.

The Mosaic Way: *A Framework for Emotionally Attuned Leadership* 2

Chapter 1   The Emotional Landscape of a Changing World 5
Chapter 2   The Erosion of Empathy 13
Chapter 3   Inner Clarity in a Noisy World 21
Chapter 4   Emotional Regulation During Chaos 31
Chapter 5   Resilience Through Motivation 39

Part II — Leading with Emotional Integrity 49

Recognize your emotions, regulate reactive impulses, and lead with grounded empathy amid uncertainty and division.

Chapter 6   The Return to Empathy 51
Chapter 7   Inclusive Social Skills for Divided Times 59
Chapter 8   Rebuilding Trust Across Differences 67

Chapter 9   Leading with Emotional Depth..............................77
Chapter 10   The Emotionally Attuned Leader in Crisis............85

Part III — Reconnecting with Others..95

Build emotionally intelligent relationships that heal, empower, and reconnect across fractures of culture and communication.

Chapter 11   Emotional Resonance for Social Justice..................97
Chapter 12   Healing Generational and Cultural Wounds........105
Chapter 13   Raising the Next Generation with
Emotional Integrity..113

Part IV — Designing the Future with EQ 123

Apply emotional intelligence to solve complex social challenges and create more inclusive, human-centered systems and spaces.

Chapter 14   Emotional Presence in the Digital Age.................125
Chapter 15   Designing Emotionally Responsive Spaces...........135
Chapter 16   Emotional Literacy and Creativity:
Finding Your Creative Voice 145
Chapter 17   Global Emotional Fluency —
Building Relationships Across Borders.........................153

**Part V — Identity, Belonging, and Emotional
            Attunement in a Global World**................................163

Explore how emotional attunement shapes identity, belonging, and leadership across cultural borders—grounded in both research and lived experience.

Chapter 18   Emotional Attunement and Identity
Formation in a Global Context 165
Chapter 19   The Conflict of Belonging —
Navigating Social Identity Across Cultures 171
Chapter 20   Reconstructing the Self —
Leadership, Culture, and Emotional Integration.........177

Part VI — The Mosaic Way™ — From Fragmented to Whole 185

Explore how emotional attunement shapes identity, belonging, and leadership across cultural borders—grounded in both research and lived experience. This section introduces the Mosaic Intelligence Method™, a human-centered framework that integrates emotional integrity, cultural flexibility, and identity agility. Through personal narratives, transformative stories, and reflective practices, this part offers a new language for inclusive leadership and a pathway to wholeness in a fragmented world.

Chapter 21: Wholeness in Action — My Mosaic Story 187

Chapter 22: The Mosaic Intelligence Method™ —
A Framework for Emotional Evolution........................191

Chapter 23: Living the Mosaic Way —
Reflections in Real Life..199

Chapter 24: The Mosaic Method's Limits —
Practicing With Integrity..209

Conclusion
*The Way Forward — Building a More Emotionally
Connected World* 213

Epilogue..217

Glossary of Key Terms 219

Discussion Guide
Reflect, Relate, Reimagine..227

Closing Note from the Author 235

Acknowledgments..237

About the Author...239

OPENING AUTHOR'S NOTE

This book emerged from disruption—personal, professional, and global. I wrote it during uncertain times, while observing the world shift in unpredictable ways that many could not yet name.

It was born out of conversations with leaders carrying silent burdens, in classrooms filled with students seeking belonging, and in quiet moments of reflection when I, too, questioned how to lead with clarity amid uncertainty.

This is not a collection of quick fixes. It is a body of work forged through lived experience, grounded in research, and guided by a deep belief: that emotional literacy is not just a skill—it is a lifeline. In seasons of rapid change, it becomes the turning point between reactive urgency and thoughtful presence, between emotional exhaustion and grounded resilience, between quiet disconnection and authentic human connection.

The Mosaic Way™ invites you to evolve—not just in how you lead others, but in how you lead yourself. It offers a new lens for emotional intelligence—one rooted in wholeness, cultural wisdom, and inclusive presence. This is a path for those who carry many stories, live at many intersections, and are ready to lead from that complexity with courage.

If you are holding this book, chances are you're navigating something unseen. You may be leading others while trying to hold yourself together, or seeking new ways to stay grounded in a world that feels increasingly unstable. I want you to know—you're not alone.

This book is for the brave.
For the reflective.
For those willing to pause, feel, and lead with heart.
This is *The Mosaic Way*.
Welcome to the journey.

— *Dr. Karissa Thomas*

FOREWORD

In an era of rapid change and disruption, *The Mosaic Way* is both timely and essential. Whether serving in the military, navigating government systems, or raising a child in a complex world, I've come to understand emotional literacy not as a privilege—but as a necessity. It is the invisible thread that weaves together strong teams, steady leadership, and secure families. Its transformative power provides both hope and direction in uncertain times.

In the Air Force, you quickly learn that you're not just a follower—you are a guide, a stabilizer, and a presence others look to in moments of instability. More than two decades of service have shown me that sound decision-making is never just about facts, protocols, or strategy. It is always about people.

Remaining calm under pressure, reading the room, and discerning when to speak or when to listen—these aren't soft skills. In high-stakes environments, they are survival skills. Self-awareness is what transforms rank into trust. I've seen people rely on their titles alone, but rank without emotional maturity doesn't inspire loyalty. Sustainable influence is built on relational intelligence, emotional steadiness, and the humility to lead without fear.

Emotional intelligence, in this context, is more than inner clarity—it's the ability to attune to others. It builds trust. It strengthens bonds. It fosters resilience under pressure. In military life, this means hearing beyond the commands, noticing what is left unsaid. I began practicing this kind of attentiveness with my team—listening not only to their words, but also to their weariness, their silence, and their invisible needs.

I remember one assignment where morale was low. The distance from home was felt in every interaction. The exhaustion was shared—and I felt it too. That deployment taught me the value of leadership rooted in connection, not just efficiency.

One of the most impactful changes we made was simple: we created a shared space. A space where we could laugh, decompress, and breathe. It wasn't fancy—but it was ours. And it changed everything.

We built it with our own hands. In doing so, we built something more. We reconnected. We remembered we weren't just units—we were human. We were a team.

That same mindset shapes how I raise my son. I often reflect on my father's absence—what he may have carried that kept him from being present for me and my brother. As a father now, I choose differently. I show up daily—with emotional presence and authenticity. A spilled drink becomes a lesson in grace. A schoolyard conflict becomes a moment to practice empathy. I teach my son to reflect before reacting, to communicate with care, and to lead with kindness. And I watch him grow into a young man who is emotionally aware—and unafraid to be.

I want him—and his generation—to understand that connection doesn't have to be complicated. Misunderstandings, fractured relationships, and divided communities often begin with emotional misalignment and poor communication. We may not always agree, but we can always choose to listen. Sometimes, the bravest thing we can do is speak truth—and create space for others to do the same.

This message matters now more than ever. The world often overlooks the human element. Social media, competition, and comparison have numbed our empathy. We judge before we understand. We ask questions to challenge—not to connect. We've forgotten how to celebrate one another without comparison.

The Mosaic Way reminds us to pause. To reflect. To respond with care. It invites us into a new way of being—one where emotional intelligence isn't just practiced, it's lived. Where leadership isn't about dominance, but about connection. Where wholeness becomes the foundation, not the exception.

We may not change the world overnight. But we can shape the next generation. I cannot control everything around me—but I can raise a son who leads with awareness, compassion, and emotional clarity.

Dr. Karissa Thomas doesn't just write about emotional fluency—she lives it. This book reflects that truth.

It calls us to lead with clarity, compassion, and connection.

It calls us to walk *The Mosaic Way*.

— Martin Scott

INTRODUCTION

Reclaiming Human Connection in a Disrupted World

There are moments in history so disruptive and irrefutably transformative that they divide time into two separate and distinct epochs: before and after. This is the moment we are experiencing. We refer to it as a pandemic, political unrest, systemic injustice, global economic volatility, environmental catastrophe, or the rising tide of technological change—but regardless of the name, it is evident that we are in the midst of a profound transformation that demands our immediate attention.

Yet many of us have failed to express the hidden cost of these disturbances: the gradual, ongoing depletion of our emotional resilience. Recognizing the emotional impact of these events is crucial, as it is a legitimate and significant aspect of our experience. However, within recognition lies the possibility for something greater—a new era of emotional resilience and intelligence, a beacon of hope in these turbulent times.

We scroll, swipe, and survive, but we rarely pause to feel, reflect, or reconnect.

We are increasingly disconnected from ourselves and one another—in boardrooms and classrooms, around dinner tables, and across digital platforms. Our attention spans are shrinking, stress levels are rising, conversations are becoming more reactive and less reflective, and compassion fatigue is a significant concern. Beneath all of this lies an undercurrent of anxiety that many have come to accept as normal. However, it is not normal, and it is certainly not sustainable.

The truth is, we are emotionally overwhelmed in a world lacking emotional fluency.

We have learned to analyze, debate, innovate, and adjust, but not how to pause, feel, empathize, or regulate our emotions. What was once dismissed as a "nice-to-have" soft skill has evolved into a vital survival competency for the twenty-first century. It has shifted from a peripheral advantage to a core requirement. Consider this as a capacity we must urgently develop to navigate the complexities of our world. It marks the difference between reaction and reflection, burnout and resilience, disconnection and deep human connection. Its importance cannot be overstated, and its relevance has never been greater.

What Is Emotional Fluency?

Emotional fluency is not just a concept; it is a practical toolbox. It encompasses awareness of our own emotions and those of others—the ability to connect through emotional awareness and the practice of attending to emotions in ways that serve rather than hinder. These are not abstract ideas; they are profoundly practical, real-world tools that help us navigate life.

They assist us in coping with stress by offering strategies to manage and overcome it. They promote healthy communication, strengthen relationships, and guide effective decision-making. These are tools that each of us can apply in our daily lives to minimize unnecessary stress and anxiety.

Yet, despite the importance of emotional skill-building, these tools are seldom prioritized in education, leadership, or policy. We often value performance metrics, technical skills, and output over emotional well-being. We reward hustle and hyper-productivity—even when they come at a significant emotional cost. However, in an era defined by disruption, those who will thrive—personally, professionally, and socially—are the ones who are emotionally grounded, adaptable, and deeply connected.

Clearly, emotional insight is not about suppressing emotions or being a pushover. Instead, it involves processing emotions wisely and developing an understanding of your inner world—allowing you to engage more intentionally with the outer world. This inner capacity equips you with the tools to bring clarity to chaos, compassion to conflict, and courage to every challenge.

Why This Book, and Why Is It Relevant Now?

My personal experiences with emotional fallout—and the harmful effects of a lack of emotional tools—have driven the creation of this book. As a consultant, educator, and leader, I have observed individuals and teams grappling with these challenges across various sectors and generations. I recognize the pattern well: intelligent, well-intentioned people often struggle under pressure—not due to a lack of knowledge or experience, but because they lack the emotional capacity to manage, respond, and rebuild connections.

Many of us were never taught how to navigate the full spectrum of our emotions. We were not shown how to resolve tension without damaging relationships. We were not guided in listening with the intent to understand rather than simply to reply. When the world around us becomes unstable, these emotional gaps widen into chasms—disrupting our ability to lead, love, and live well. You are not alone in this struggle. We are all in this together; this book is a testament to that.

This book is not merely a theoretical exploration of emotional fluency; it serves as a practical guide and leadership toolkit designed to address the emotional voids we often encounter. It provides tools to navigate real-world emotions while evolving into an inclusive leader. In today's world, emotional depth transcends self-mastery—it forms the foundation of leadership that fosters belonging, honors diversity, and builds bridges across differences. It equips you to manage and regulate your emotions effectively, empowering you to take charge of your emotional well-being while leading with greater impact and integrity.

It is neither a textbook, a memoir, nor a conventional leadership manual. Instead, it is an unprecedented roadmap that intertwines research, lived experience, and actionable insights. It serves as a relevant, real-world guide for anyone seeking emotional clarity in an age shrouded in confusion—and as a vital resource for fostering meaningful connections in an increasingly disconnected time.

Throughout these pages, you will discover how to identify your emotional triggers, manage challenging emotions, communicate with greater empathy, and foster trust-based relationships—even in environments where misunderstanding and emotional distance often prevail. You will also learn how to embody emotional presence in real-life contexts, strengthening your capacity to guide others with clarity and care. These insights will expand your influence and deepen your understanding across diverse domains—including education, business, social justice movements, and community life.

The High Cost of Lacking Emotional Connection

Before we can reclaim emotional depth, we must first comprehend what is missing in its absence. This understanding empowers us to take action—to restore this vital aspect of our shared humanity.

Reflect on your last heated meeting, where tensions ran high and voices were raised. Consider the last conversation in which you felt unheard—the frustration, the disappointment, and the silent retreat that followed. Imagine scrolling through social media in the wake of a tragedy, only to encounter performative outrage instead of genuine shared grief. The emotional toll of these moments is real, and they represent only a fraction of the disconnection we face in our modern world.

These experiences do not occur in a vacuum; they are symptoms of a deep inner drought—a depletion of the emotional resources and relational skills necessary to navigate life with wisdom and care. If left unaddressed, this drought can lead to a relational wasteland. In this barren landscape, the tools required to mend our relationships—with ourselves, our children, our partners, and the world—are either absent or overlooked. Recognizing and addressing our emotional needs is essential to prevent such outcomes. Without this awareness, communication fractures, conflict escalates, innovation stagnates, collaboration falters, and trust—arguably the most valuable currency in any relationship—is easily lost.

When organizations are led by individuals with low emotional capacity and staffed by emotionally disconnected workers, the outcome is often high turnover rates and toxic workplace cultures. Research indicates that employees whose managers demonstrate high levels of emotional fluency are four times less likely to resign compared to those whose managers lack it. Furthermore, a study found that eighty percent of Gen Z and Millennial workers would contemplate leaving their jobs because of a toxic work environment. This is not merely a problem; it is a crisis.

When emotional awareness is absent in families, it can lead to fractured relationships, broken homes, and the perpetuation of intergenerational trauma. In our communities, its lack breeds division, dehumanization, and a collective resistance to the healing conversations we desperately need.

We all have a role in turning the tide, and meaningful progress is within reach. We can no longer afford to live in a world that relegates emotional development to the realm of the "soft" or undervalues its transformative power. The time to act is now.

Disruption Is Not Going Away—
But We Can Respond Differently

One of the hardest truths to accept is that disruption is here to stay. We cannot simply wait this out. Things are not going back to the way they were, and in many ways, we may not want them to.

This reality demands a deeper form of evolution: emotional, spiritual, and social.

We are entering a new epoch, and with it comes the need for a new skill set—one grounded in emotional agility, radical empathy, cultural humility, and collective responsibility. We must learn to feel without becoming overwhelmed, to connect without compromising our identity, and to disagree in ways that preserve dignity rather than dehumanize. The journey to develop these skills may be difficult, but it is also transformative. It is a path illuminated by hope, courage, and the promise of a better tomorrow.

This work is not easy, but it is necessary.

The good news is this: we can grow our emotional insight and leadership capacity over time. Relational fluency is accessible to everyone—whether you are a chief executive officer, teacher, parent, activist, artist, or student. It is not fixed or limited by personality or circumstance. It begins with intention. As you grow, so does your capacity to recognize the diverse emotional patterns—both your own and those of others—that form what I call the **Mosaic Intelligence Method**™: the ability to lead with emotional integrity, cultural flexibility, and identity agility in a rapidly shifting world.

What This Book Can Offer You

This book is structured into six parts that take you on a progressive journey—from emotional survival in a disrupted world to embodied, inclusive leadership rooted in emotional fluency and cultural integrity.

Each section builds upon the last, guiding you through inner clarity, relational healing, and ultimately, the integration of a new leadership model: the Mosaic Intelligence Method™.

Part I: The Emotional Landscape of Our Time

We explore how rapid societal shifts affect our emotional well-being, and why emotional fluency—not just intelligence—has become a necessary survival skill in the age of constant disruption.

Part II: Leading with Emotional Integrity

This section invites you to deepen your self-awareness, regulate your inner world, and respond to uncertainty with grounded clarity and compassion. You will learn to lead from within, not perform from expectation.

Part III: Reconnecting with Others

Here we focus on relationships. You will rediscover empathy, develop attuned communication, and cultivate emotionally safe spaces across divides of culture, history, and experience.

Part IV: Designing the Future with EQ

Emotional intelligence becomes a tool for structural transformation—applied to digital life, creative expression, and the redesign of institutions. You'll explore how emotional fluency shapes innovation, equity, and healing systems.

Part V: Identity, Belonging, and Emotional Attunement in a Global World

Drawing from both lived experience and doctoral research, this section examines how emotional literacy intersects with identity development, belonging, and cultural adaptability. You'll explore how to lead across borders and differences with authenticity and humility.

Part VI: The Mosaic Way™ —
From Fragmented to Whole

This final section introduces the Mosaic Intelligence Method™—a new framework for leading through fragmentation with clarity, compassion, and cultural fluency. Through personal narrative, real-world stories, and reflective practices, you'll discover a pathway for integrated leadership that is both deeply personal and globally relevant.

Each chapter contains stories, research, reflective prompts, and practical tools—not to dictate how you feel, but to assist you in understanding why you feel the way you do, what to do with those emotions, and how to grow through them.

This book serves as both a mirror and a map: a mirror that allows you to see yourself more clearly, and a map that guides you toward a life marked by emotional fluency and relational depth.

The Invitation

Emotional resonance is not about perfection—it's about being present: more attuned, more compassionate, more human.

We are not designed to navigate life feeling numb, defensive, or disconnected. We are meant to feel deeply, connect meaningfully, and create change through care. However, doing so requires us to slow down, listen, unlearn, and make different choices.

You might be holding this book because something in your life feels out of balance. Perhaps you are a leader who has started to notice emotional gaps within your team, family, or community. Or maybe you are weary of the noise, conflict, and disconnection and are ready to try something new.

If that is the case, you are in the right place.

This is not a quick fix; it is a journey—a conscious decision to meet yourself and others with greater honesty and grace. It entails a commitment to building a life—and a world—rooted in emotional grounding, cultural humility, and meaningful connection.

Allow that commitment to guide you. Let it influence how you present yourself.

Now is the moment to take the first step. Together.

Exploring and Embracing the Landscape of Disruption

You were never meant to navigate life in disconnection. You were created to feel profoundly, to lead with intention, and to move through this world aware of what truly matters.

This is your invitation to return—

to your voice,

to your wisdom,

to your power,

to your whole self.

Allow clarity to guide you. Allow compassion to shape you.

Allow emotional availability to become your new mode of being.

This marks the beginning of something sacred.

You are not merely reading a book; you are transforming into something more.

PART I

THE EMOTIONAL LANDSCAPE OF OUR TIME

We are experiencing unprecedented levels of disruption. This section explores how emotional resonance aids us in navigating disconnection, uncertainty, and the noise of modern life. Each chapter offers tools for staying grounded, present, and resilient in a world that rarely slows down.

Dr. Karissa Thomas

The Mosaic Way
A New Language for Leadership

Why Mosaic?

We live in fragmented times.

Disruption is no longer the exception—it's the atmosphere. Cultural collisions, generational divides, shifting identities, and rapid technological acceleration have reshaped how we lead, relate, and understand ourselves.

Traditional emotional intelligence gave us tools to navigate emotion—but often lacked the language for complexity, the nuance to lead across cultures, and the courage to evolve our identities in real time.

That's why the Mosaic Intelligence Method™ was born.

More than a framework, it's a philosophy—a new way of leading that embraces emotional wholeness in a world that often rewards fragmentation.

The Mosaic Way invites leaders to cultivate:

Emotional Integrity — aligning what you feel, value, and do.

Cultural Flexibility — adapting without erasing who you are.

Identity Agility — leading from a self that is evolving, expansive, and rooted.

This book is not a manual. It's a mirror, a map, and a movement. It will ask you to slow down, reflect deeply, and lead differently.

Not because emotional intelligence is obsolete—but because it's time for it to evolve.

Inclusive leadership is not a separate outcome of the Mosaic Intelligence Method™—it is its essence. When we lead with emotional integrity, cultural flexibility, and identity agility, we create environments where people of all backgrounds feel seen, valued, and emotionally safe. These pillars offer a practical path to inclusive spaces grounded in dignity and shared humanity.

What Is the Mosaic Intelligence Method™?

The Mosaic Intelligence Method™ is an evolution of emotional intelligence—crafted for a fragmented, fast-moving, and culturally complex world.

While traditional EQ focuses on managing emotions, Mosaic Intelligence expands that capacity into three integrated dimensions:

Emotional Integrity — cultivating coherence between inner emotion, core values, and outward action.

Cultural Flexibility — skillfully navigating across cultural, generational, and social contexts while remaining authentically yourself.

Identity Agility — leading from a dynamic sense of self that honors change without losing center.

This method helps you lead through contradiction, ambiguity, and change—not by simplifying complexity, but by becoming more whole within it.

Who This Book Is For:
Three Pathways to Emotional Fluency

This book is designed to meet you exactly where you are—and guide you into deeper emotional presence, relational influence, and meaningful connection. Whether you're navigating leadership roles, caregiving responsibilities, or your own personal growth, the tools and insights in these pages will resonate with your journey. Here's how you might engage with them:

For Those Guiding Others: You'll find practices to cultivate emotionally safe, high-trust environments—whether in boardrooms, classrooms, or community spaces. This book equips you to lead with clarity instead of control, and to move teams through complexity with grounded presence.

For Educators, Parents, and Caregivers: You'll uncover ways to model emotional literacy, foster authentic communication, and nurture attuned children and students. These strategies help you move beyond reaction and into responsive, relationship-centered care.

For Everyday Navigators: Whether you're working through personal healing, managing workplace tension, or seeking deeper self-understanding, this book offers practices that reconnect you to your own wisdom—and help you show up with grounded clarity in every space you enter.

No matter your title, this book is a companion in your evolution. The language of emotional fluency belongs to all of us—and your presence in these pages is part of reshaping what guidance, care, and connection can look like in today's world.

CHAPTER 1

The Emotional Landscape of a Changing World

There was a time when disruption felt temporary. It arrived in waves—wars, recessions, natural disasters—events that shook us, then passed. Life moved forward with stretches of predictability, punctuated by moments that required adaptation and healing. But something has shifted.

Disruption is no longer merely an interruption; it is the constant backdrop of our lives. It shapes our headlines, homes, health, and humanity. What was once an exception has now become the norm. We are no longer navigating a single crisis—we are managing multiple layers of uncertainty simultaneously: global pandemics, political division, climate disasters, mass shootings, financial instability, cultural fragmentation, and a technological revolution that is outpacing our ethical considerations.

These disruptions are not distant—they shape how we show up at work, how we engage with loved ones, and how we even see ourselves. A teacher may be balancing hybrid classrooms, ailing parents, and racial trauma all at once. A manager may be expected to inspire their team while quietly grieving a personal loss. In this compounded context, emotional fatigue doesn't feel like a breakdown—it feels like the new baseline.

The crisis of emotional disconnection is no longer emerging—it has become urgent. It demands our immediate awareness.

The Era of Compound Crises

This is the new normal, and we are exhausted—not just physically but emotionally and spiritually. Many of us are functioning but not flourishing, connected yet lonely, busy yet directionless.

In this reality, emotional fluency is not only helpful—it is essential. It provides clarity in the fog and connection amid the fragmentation.

Sociologists and psychologists characterize this era as one of compounded crises or cascading disruptions. Instead of facing isolated challenges, we are experiencing crises that layer and intertwine, triggering each other in unpredictable ways. A health emergency causes economic fallout. A political conflict sparks social unrest. A climate disaster results in housing insecurity. And through it all, people are expected to endure.

This relentless pace of trauma, transition, and tension does not come without consequence. Rates of anxiety, depression, and burnout are rising worldwide. The World Health Organization reported a twenty-five percent increase in anxiety and depression during the pandemic, yet the figures reflect a deeper unraveling—one that began long before the virus and continues long after.

Why Emotional Depth Matters Now More Than Ever

In seasons of uncertainty, emotional fluency becomes more than a skill—it becomes our grounding force. It is the quiet strength that steadies us, allowing us to respond rather than react, to connect rather than control, and to lead with emotional grounding rather than pressure. When the world feels unstable, this inner wisdom anchors us in what we can regulate: our internal landscape.

This emotional insight helps us stay grounded even when everything around us is shifting. It enables us to face difficult realities with clarity, to respond rather than react, and to offer compassion even when the world feels overwhelming. It is the language of connection, the practice of authenticity, and the foundation of resilient leadership.

The Cost of Emotional Fragmentation

If the headlines capture our attention, another crisis is quietly unfolding within: emotional fragmentation. We are bombarded by bad news and unmet expectations. We are flooded with information but deprived of meaning. We are surrounded by others, yet feel profoundly alone. Many of us exist in a state of emotional dissonance—appearing fine on the outside while feeling fractured on the inside.

I remember speaking with a frontline nurse who described how she could handle the patient load, the shift changes, and even the grief—but what exhausted her most was the emotional contradiction. "One minute I'm holding someone's hand while they take their last breath," she said, "and the next I'm expected to answer an insurance email as if nothing happened." That dissonance—the emotional multitasking of survival—has become a common, invisible strain.

Some of us feel numb, while others are hyper-reactive. Many simply do not know how to feel at all. This fragmentation manifests everywhere—in families as irritability or withdrawal, in workplaces as miscommunication and burnout, and in leadership as paralysis or poor decision-making.

The good news is that emotional depth provides a way forward. It teaches us to integrate instead of fragment. To feel rather than avoid. To lead with authenticity rather than performance.

Looking Beyond the Myth of Constant Productivity

One of the most harmful beliefs of our time is the notion that our value is linked to our productivity. Even as the world crumbles around us, we are urged to rise and grind, to show up and perform, to succeed at any cost. We take pride in functioning under pressure—but functioning does not equate to flourishing. Many of us are functioning in emotional overdraft—giving from a point of depletion and leading from survival, not strength.

Leadership today is more emotionally complex than ever. It is not just about managing workflows; it involves managing fear, fatigue, trauma, and hope. Leading in this era requires more than competence; it demands consciousness.

It involves reading emotional cues, creating space for discomfort, and providing guidance while acknowledging the pain. Whether you lead a team, a classroom, a family, or a movement, this moment urges you to lead with both mind and heart. It was never meant to be a weakness. This is relational wisdom in motion.

Letting Go of the Fantasy of Normality

One of the most seductive illusions of recent years has been the idea of returning to "normal." After the initial shock of global disruption, many clung to the hope that life would resume as it was before—that we could bounce back untouched and unchanged. However, "normal" was never emotionally sustainable. It was often inequitable, disconnected, and driven by systems that prioritized speed over sustainability. What we need is not a return—but a reinvention.

A new normal must be emotionally aware. One where well-being is a priority, where rest is valued as much as results, and where connection takes precedence over control. We are not going back. But we can move forward—intentionally, emotionally, and together.

Emotional Literacy as Our Compass

If disruption is the context, emotional fluency serves as the compass. It allows us to navigate uncertainty with clarity, lead with compassion, and respond to challenges without losing ourselves. It empowers the teacher to de-escalate a classroom through connection rather than punishment. The executive navigates crisis with empathy instead of fear. The parent remains grounded through a child's storm. The community holds one another through collective grief.

This emotional capacity empowers us to recognize what is broken while nurturing what is whole. It allows us to access hope—not as a passive feeling, but as a grounded vision.

In the chapters ahead, we will explore the five core components of emotional mastery: self-awareness, self-regulation, intrinsic motivation, empathy, and social skills. However, before we practice these, we must accept this truth: the world is changing, and the most significant transformation we can achieve is internal.

Reclaiming Ourselves in the Midst of Chaos

When your surroundings are unstable, your greatest strength lies in reclaiming what is within. You do not need all the answers or to be perfect. You simply need to be present—emotionally aware, willing to reflect, and open to growth. This is where anchored leadership takes root.

This is the work of being more human in a system that rewards performance over authenticity. It is the sacred act of reclaiming your clarity, your calm, and your capacity to feel. Emotional resilience is not discovered outside the storm—it is forged within it.

The Emotional Cry in the Workplace

As I travel, speak, and consult across industries, I hear a silent cry echoing through corporate strategy decks, all-hands meetings, and wellness initiatives: People are emotionally exhausted.

Employees are arriving depleted—not because they lack concern, but because they are running on empty. Employers are struggling to support their teams in an environment that rewards output while neglecting emotional reality.

It is not just the workforce. I have sat across from executives, managers, and human resource leaders carrying the invisible weight of doing more with less. They are trying to protect their teams while staying afloat in a culture that values speed but punishes slowness. Many are strong, capable, and compassionate. However, they are also overwhelmed, emotionally fatigued, and often too burdened to recognize it.

This is the cry of leadership in an age of relentless change. It is not solely about productivity; it is about people striving to remain human in systems that rarely pause. The increase in requests for emotional fluency training is not a mere trend; it is a call for transformation. Organizations are realizing they can no longer ignore the emotional climate of their teams. They bring me in not just for workshops, but for healing.

And I have seen what occurs when people are provided with tools to articulate their feelings, when language takes the place of silence, and when leadership is demonstrated with empathy and accountability—something shifts.

Where does responsibility lie: with the employer or the employee? The answer is both.

Leaders must build cultures that prioritize psychological safety, inner clarity, and rest. Individuals must also take ownership of mindset, emotional regulation, and relational well-being.

I have witnessed the result: teams do not transform because the workload disappears, but because they learn to manage energy, process emotion, and lead from awareness. I have watched leaders cry, not from burnout, but from breakthrough. I have seen individuals reclaim agency, recover connection, and rebuild their sense of purpose because they finally felt seen.

This is what I do; this is my calling.

This is what happens when we stop pushing people beyond their limits and start creating cultures that rejuvenate them.

Reflection

THE EMOTIONAL LANDSCAPE OF A CHANGING WORLD

When disruption becomes the backdrop of everyday life, it is easy to normalize disconnection from our inner world. This reflection marks the beginning of a deeper journey—one that invites you to reclaim clarity, intention, and grounded presence in an ever-shifting world.

- Where in your life are you operating on autopilot instead of flourishing with intention?
- What systems or environments have conditioned you to prioritize productivity over emotional authenticity?
- What version of "normal" are you being asked to release in order to lead more consciously?

Transformation does not begin with a perfect plan.
It begins with honest awareness.

CHAPTER 2

The Erosion of Empathy

Empathy—the ability to understand and share another person's feelings—has long been a cornerstone of relational awareness. It bridges difference, anchors us in community, and drives our collective pursuit of justice, compassion, and healing. Yet today, empathy is slipping through our fingers.

The Erosion of Compassionate Connection

We are witnessing a quiet erosion of compassion. The signs are all around us: deepening division, rising incivility, outrage-driven media, performative call-outs, and a growing numbness to the pain of others. In workplaces, emotional awareness is too often eclipsed by productivity metrics. In classrooms, connection is sacrificed for content coverage. In politics, complexity is flattened into slogans. And in everyday life, we are frequently too weary to care—or too distracted to even notice.

This is not a passing trend. When we lose emotional attunement, relational intelligence suffers. It becomes self-serving rather than connective, strategic rather than sincere, and performative instead of transformative. In an age of rapid change, emotional presence is no longer a soft skill—it is a survival skill.

Compassion in Decline: A Measurable Crisis

The erosion of compassion is not merely a philosophical concern—it is measurable and urgent. A comprehensive study by researchers at the University of Michigan analyzed data from nearly fourteen thousand college students between 1979 and 2009, revealing a forty percent decline in empathy—with the most significant drop occurring in the 2000s. More recently, a 2023 report by the American Psychological Association found that nearly sixty percent of young adults say they feel emotionally disconnected even when surrounded by others, citing digital overload, performance pressure, and social fragmentation as key drivers. These findings confirm what many sense intuitively: both cognitive empathy—the ability to understand another's perspective—and emotional empathy—the capacity to feel what someone else is feeling—are diminishing under the weight of emotional fatigue and cultural distraction.

Digital Distance, Genuine Disconnection

Technology has brought us closer together—and further apart.

We can send messages across the world in seconds, yet struggle to be emotionally present with the person beside us. Digital spaces reward outrage over reflection and elevate visibility over vulnerability. We're celebrated for likes and shares, but rarely for listening and understanding.

Text messages have replaced real conversations, while emojis stand in for genuine emotion. In the process, we lose something vital: attunement—the capacity to feel with and for others.

Even video calls, which became a lifeline during the pandemic, can leave us emotionally drained. Research from Stanford University's Virtual Human Interaction Lab confirms that the artificial mimicry of eye contact, the absence of natural social cues, and constant self-monitoring on screen all contribute to mental and emotional fatigue.

This disconnection has real consequences—especially in leadership and education.

Leaders who become digitally distant lose the emotional pulse of their teams. Educators who teach through screens without true engagement often find their students passive, detached, and unmotivated. And when we spend more time curating our digital presence than cultivating our inner lives, empathy shifts from being personal to being performative.

In today's hyper-visible culture, empathy is increasingly packaged as content. A manager may engage with mental health content online while ignoring signs of burnout on their team. An influencer may share raw reflections about trauma while silencing dissenting voices in their comments. These moments—though wrapped in the language of care—can feel hollow when not grounded in relational depth.

When empathy becomes a brand strategy instead of a bridge, it loses its capacity to transform—and becomes a tool of disconnection.

Empathy vs. Outrage Culture

The rise of outrage culture has eroded our collective empathy. In a time shaped by emotional extremes and rapid judgment, feelings are wielded like weapons instead of held with care. We are pushed to choose sides, draw hard lines, and define others by their worst moments or most provocative words.

Outrage may feel powerful, but it is no match for emotional attunement. While outrage declares, "I am right, and you are wrong," attunement inquires, "Help me understand how you see this." Outrage isolates, whereas attunement builds bridges.

Dr. Brené Brown reminds us, "People are hard to hate close up. Move in." Moving in requires emotional courage. It involves listening to those with whom we disagree. It entails staying curious when judgment is easier. It requires holding space for discomfort without rushing to solve it. Outrage may burn brightly, but empathy creates lasting light.

The Cost of Compassion Fatigue

Another reason empathy is fading is that we are emotionally exhausted. The human heart is not built to carry every global tragedy, every social injustice, and every personal burden simultaneously. Over time, constant exposure to suffering can result in emotional shutdown.

This state—referred to as compassion fatigue—was initially identified in healthcare, but it now applies to anyone enduring prolonged emotional stress. It does not arise from indifference; rather, it emerges from depletion.

Compassion fatigue manifests as cynicism, detachment, or emotional numbness. It occurs when caregivers, educators, leaders, and activists give without replenishing themselves. This condition poses one of the greatest threats to sustained empathy.

A 2019 study published in Clinical Psychological Science found that individuals who suppress or ignore emotional stress are significantly more likely to experience burnout and reduced empathy. In simple terms: we cannot pour from an empty vessel. Empathy requires emotional fuel—and far too many of us are running on empty.

Leaders Establish the Emotional Atmosphere

Emotional presence begins with personal insight but flourishes within culture—and culture is shaped by leadership. Whether you are a CEO, a principal, a team leader, or a parent, you establish the emotional climate of the spaces you oversee. By modeling attunement—through listening, validating, and connecting—you foster environments where others feel safe to do the same.

In times of deep transition, people need more than answers—they need to feel seen. They need leaders who can hold emotional complexity, remain steady amid uncertainty, and recognize that validation—not agreement—is often the most powerful form of support. Relational leadership is not soft; it is strategic. It cultivates trust, invites authenticity, and creates cultures where people are free to be whole.

Restoring Connection in a Disconnected World

Attunement is not an inherited trait; it is a skill—one that can be practiced and strengthened. Restoring relational depth in a disconnected world begins with intentional authenticity. It starts by slowing down, tuning in, and acknowledging our own emotional experience so that we can better engage with the emotions of others.

Listening is one of the most powerful tools in your emotional toolkit—but it must be done with the intent to understand, not merely to respond. Ask open-ended questions. Stay curious. Allow silence to stretch long enough to invite honesty.

We restore connection by replacing judgment with curiosity. Judgment shuts down understanding; curiosity invites it. Just as important are emotional boundaries: attunement does not mean emotional absorption. It means being fully present—without losing yourself. True empathy requires boundaries. Without them, care becomes codependence, and compassion becomes exhaustion. Empathy asks us to feel *with*, not *for*—to witness pain without becoming it. This distinction preserves the sustainability of our care. We are not called to carry every emotion, but to companion it with dignity. Boundaries make emotional availability sustainable.

Above all, we must prioritize connection. Conversations matter. Emotional presence matters. Compassion does not require grand gestures; it only requires care. When extended with integrity and presence, even the smallest act can become a moment of healing.

The Future Belongs to the Empathetic

In a world increasingly shaped by artificial intelligence, emotional depth will become our greatest distinction. Empathy is not a relic of the past; it is a revolutionary force for the future. It allows us to build bridges rather than walls, to lead with integrity instead of ego, and to heal with understanding rather than shame. We are not powerless in the face of disconnection; we can choose empathy—in our families, in our schools, in our workplaces, and in our communities. And we can begin today.

Lessons on Daily Compassion

Small acts of empathy now carry extraordinary significance in a world that feels faster, louder, and more detached. Compassion has emerged as a quiet form of resistance—an intentional choice to stay human in environments that often neglect to be.

It is the grocery clerk who says, "Take your time." It is the nurse who explains patiently. It is the receptionist who observes your fatigue and offers a kind word. These moments, once commonplace, now feel sacred.

I have witnessed this firsthand—not only as a coach and consultant but also while working in catastrophe claims, deployed during some of the most devastating hurricanes and floods in recent years. In neighborhoods still recovering from shock, where policyholders are trying to manage both paperwork and grief, I have seen that it is not always the most efficient or technically skilled professionals who create the greatest impact. It is those who lead with compassion.

I remember one customer service representative who encountered a policyholder in distress, anger, and overwhelm. Instead of rushing through the process, she paused to listen and acknowledged his fear. That simple act shifted the entire tone of the interaction. Although his losses remained, his dignity was restored.

These moments are not only meaningful; they are also transformative. Research confirms that compassion-centered communication reduces emotional stress and enhances satisfaction, particularly in high-stress environments. More than seventy percent of employees report that being treated with respect is more important than recognition or bonuses.

We are wired for empathy. In its absence, we disengage. Today, those who choose to lead with care—especially when it is not required—stand out. They anchor us. Their kindness may go unspoken, but it is often the reason someone manages to get through the day.

For years, harshness left the deepest mark. Now, it fades quickly. What remains is kindness.

In a culture hungry for connection, leaders who embody emotional fluency and relational wisdom are not just necessary—they are revolutionary. To those who continue to lead with care in a world that often forgets to express gratitude: thank you.

You are not merely kind; you are emotionally attuned, and you are shaping the future of leadership in this new era of humanity.

Reflection

THE EROSION OF EMPATHY

As emotional fatigue increases, emotional attunement is often the first quality to erode and the last to be recognized as missing. These questions help raise awareness of how emotional presence is expressed, safeguarded, or neglected in both personal and professional environments.

- Where have you noticed your emotional responsiveness being replaced by fatigue, judgment, or detachment?
- How has technology shaped the way you connect—or disconnect—from the emotions of others?
- In what space or relationship are you being invited to lead with deeper compassion, even if it feels inconvenient?
- In what spaces have you withheld empathy because of unfamiliarity, bias, or emotional fatigue—and what would it look like to re-engage those spaces with curiosity and care?
- How does your inner clarity help others feel emotionally safe or culturally seen?

Relational attunement is not an extra. It is the bridge that holds our humanity together.

CHAPTER 3

Inner Clarity in a Noisy World

In every era of change, there comes a moment when we must stop looking outward and begin looking inward. That moment is now. We live in a world saturated with sound—news, opinions, updates, algorithms, and expectations—so much so that it becomes easy to lose sight of the quiet truth of who we truly are. The external noise often drowns out our inner voice. Emotional noise is like static on an old radio—constant, crackling, and relentless. It blurs the signal of who we truly are until all that's left is distortion.

Clarity, on the other hand, is the quiet hum beneath the chaos—the steady signal we can return to if we learn to tune back in. It doesn't compete for attention; it waits for presence. Yet emotional regulation begins with inner clarity, and inner clarity starts with silence, pause, and stillness.

Uncovering your true self beneath the noise is not just an act of emotional leadership; it's a profound journey of self-empowerment. This journey equips you with the clarity and purpose needed to navigate life's complexities.

The Lost Art of Self-Discovery

True inner insight means recognizing your emotions and motivations with curiosity and compassion—then applying that understanding to how you lead and relate. It involves viewing yourself with openness and grace—and using that clarity in your relationships and decisions.

According to research by Tasha Eurich, author of *Insight*, while ninety-five percent of people believe they are self-aware, only ten to fifteen percent truly are. This gap, though significant, is not insurmountable. Through the transformative power of emotional insight, we can bridge that gap and live with greater intention and consciousness.

This disconnect is most striking during times of disruption—when leaders are most needed. However, through reflective awareness, we uncover patterns of reassurance, understanding, and growth, enabling us to lead with clarity even in the eye of the storm.

The Noise Is Not Just External—It Is Internal

The modern world does not just distract us—it drowns us. Amid social media feeds, endless news cycles, digital expectations, and curated identities, we find ourselves surrounded by mirrors that reflect everything but our true selves. Gradually, we start to confuse noise with truth.

Even our inner dialogue turns into a recycled loop of external voices: family expectations, cultural conditioning, generational beliefs, and unprocessed trauma. These narratives quietly shape our interpretation of the world—and our self-definition.

To calm the internal storm, we must practice deliberate inner reflection. This starts by asking difficult, often uncomfortable questions: What am I truly reacting to right now? What narrative am I telling myself at this moment? Who am I showing up as—and is that someone I respect?

These are not casual reflections; they are foundational inquiries. The answers unveil the emotional algorithms from which we unconsciously operate. Once we examine them with honesty, we can start to rewrite them—with intention, clarity, and compassion.

Emphasizing Presence Over Perfection: The Essence of Cross-Cultural Connection

Cultural self-insight is as vital as emotional understanding. The better we grasp our own cultural perspective, the more we can respect and collaborate with those who perceive the world in different ways.

In business, this involves understanding the nuances of cross-cultural communication. In some cultures, direct confrontation is avoided, and disagreements are managed more subtly. In relationships, it entails avoiding assumptions and embracing differences with kindness and openness. While some cultures express emotions openly, others consider emotional restraint a sign of respect. Recognizing these differences helps us navigate relationships more effectively.

Cultural attunement is at the heart of global leadership. It involves the ability to comprehend and manage emotions across multicultural contexts. It begins with recognizing one's own emotional patterns and those of others, then extends to applying that awareness to navigate diverse environments with humility and grace.

This level of emotional fluency acknowledges that although emotions are universal, their expression and interpretation vary across cultures. It is not about abandoning your identity, but about refining how you show up—so that your presence strengthens, rather than fractures, connection.

Such intercultural emotional skill transcends borders and generations. It shapes how we work, lead, love, and foster authentic connections. We will explore this more deeply in Chapter Seventeen.

Generational Echoes: Inner Awareness Through Time

Personal insight varies between generations, with each carrying its unique emotional legacy.

Baby Boomers were often raised in environments that prioritized stoicism, duty, and structure. Emotions were to be managed, not explored. For many, the journey inward begins by unlearning silence and giving themselves permission to feel.

Generation X grew up as quiet observers—navigating shifting norms, latchkey independence, and the tail end of analog life. They became emotionally self-reliant out of necessity, often developing resilience without language for their inner worlds. Their insight often emerges through reflection, reinvention, and the long arc of self-trust.

Millennials entered adulthood amid economic uncertainty, the rise of digital life, and increasing openness around mental health. They are fluent in the language of self-expression but often carry the weight of comparison and burnout. Their pursuit of clarity includes untangling performance from worth, and expression from identity.

Generation Z is coming of age in a hyper-connected, emotionally expressive, and socially urgent world. They are quick to name their feelings but may lack the tools to regulate them. Their challenge lies not in access to emotion—but in processing it with depth, stillness, and discernment.

Emotional grounding is a universal need, but the path to it is shaped by culture, conditioning, and context. Each generation is both responding to the past and shaping the future. The invitation is not to perfect emotional awareness—but to deepen it together, across time, in community.

The Imperative of Inner Clarity

Inner clarity is the cornerstone of trust. When those in positions of influence cultivate both self-awareness and emotional transparency, they create environments where people feel seen, safe, and supported. This kind of grounded presence transforms not only culture—but also capacity.

Leaders who are grounded in self-awareness are hard to find—but more necessary than ever. Their impact is shaped not just by insight, but by emotional regulation: the disciplined ability to pause, reflect, and respond instead of react.

Relational influence goes beyond directing others. It requires awareness of how your groundedness shapes a room, how your energy affects others, and how your blind spots may unintentionally distort outcomes. Even with good intentions, a lack of internal clarity can create ripple effects of harm.

People don't follow titles—they follow presence.

When relational stewards lead with emotional honesty, teams trust more deeply. They model humility, embrace vulnerability, and create space for others to show up fully. These emotionally fluent spaces cultivate psychological safety, where individuals feel free to express themselves honestly and engage meaningfully.

The cost of unaware guidance is immense. According to the *Harvard Business Review*, organizations guided by reflective decision-makers tend to be more profitable, innovative, and resilient. Self-insight fosters transparency, adaptability, and compassion—qualities that cannot be automated or outsourced.

Noise is the sound of influence without reflection. Resonance, on the other hand, begins with internal alignment. The difference isn't in volume—it's in emotional depth.

Practicing Inner Awareness in a Chaotic World

Emotional clarity is not a destination; it is a daily decision, a practice, and a way of being. Choosing grounded awareness—even when it feels uncomfortable—has the power to transform your life.

There are simple and accessible ways to build this awareness. Think of clarity as a rhythm rather than a resolution. It is nurtured through small, sacred acts: a daily moment of breath before opening your inbox, a short walk without headphones, a morning journal entry with no audience. These moments are not indulgent—they are insurgent. In a world addicted to noise, they reclaim your inner signal. Start by creating intentional pauses throughout your day. Before reacting, take a breath and ask yourself, "What am I feeling? Why?" That brief moment of reflection can change everything.

Journaling can also be a powerful practice. You don't need eloquence—just honesty. Use your reflections to identify patterns, explore emotional triggers, and gain clarity over time.

Seek feedback by asking someone you trust, "What is it like to be on the other side of me?" Then listen—not to defend, but to understand. This level of emotional maturity fosters true growth.

Notice your reactions—especially the intense ones. They often indicate past wounds or unfulfilled needs. Use this insight not to criticize yourself but to explore with kindness.

Finally, clarify your values. Knowing what truly matters to you helps your decisions align more naturally, making your life feel more purposeful. Growth isn't about idealization; it's about progress, grounded awareness, and allowing yourself to evolve.

It is a journey, and you are already on your way.

From Self-Awareness to Self-Guidance

Self-awareness is the birthplace of personal guidance. Knowing how to direct your own energy—especially when no one else can—is the foundation of meaningful influence. This is the heart of inner awareness and intentional action: the ability to recognize your emotional patterns, regulate your internal state, and align your decisions with your values under pressure.

It enables you to establish boundaries that protect your peace, communicate in ways that build trust, and adapt with purpose. Most importantly, it empowers you to model emotional courage in how you show up for others.

Self-guidance is the quiet strength behind intentional living and relational influence. It is what transforms awareness into presence—and presence into power.

The world does not need more noise; it needs more grounded, reflective, and emotionally mature individuals who understand themselves and live from that clarity. When anchored in inner discernment, you remain unshakeable in the storm. You become a safe space for others and a mirror—not of confusion, but of clarity.

Lessons from Dubai: A Global Perspective on Self-Awareness

Living in Dubai during one of its most transformative periods taught me that growth requires self-reflection. The city was evolving rapidly—fast, global, and ambitious. Yet with every gleaming skyscraper came a deeper tension: tradition versus progress, identity versus reinvention.

As a Western American woman, I had to rediscover myself. Immersed in an Eastern culture that demanded humility, adaptation, and introspection, I quickly realized that what worked in New York, Texas, or Los Angeles did not always translate to Dubai. This mismatch compelled me to listen, observe, and reflect more deeply. The culture not only challenged me externally; it also required me to evolve internally.

In the West, we are conditioned to prioritize freedom and expression. In the East, collective harmony, reverence, and restraint are often more deeply valued. Navigating these differences has taught me that inner awareness is not static—it is contextual. It expands when we step outside our norms and deepens when we are willing to unlearn.

That growth did not happen overnight. It took nearly two years to consistently and authentically engage and build trust with the Emiratis alongside whom I worked. I had to deconstruct aspects of myself rooted in performance, transactions, or hyper-independence—not because they were wrong, but because they no longer supported the deeper connections I was trying to cultivate.

I had to relearn how to be emotionally available in a space that was less familiar, more nuanced, and rooted in values that challenged my perspective. I learned that trust is not only earned; it is revealed—through groundedness, consistency, and humility.

Sometimes, I became quiet—not because I had nothing to say, but because I was learning to listen without needing to take charge. Other times, I was misunderstood—and I had to learn not to defend myself, but to reflect. Over time, the relationships deepened and became more honest—not because I tried to fit in, but because I allowed myself to be fully seen, with both cultural respect and emotional maturity.

Cultural insight is as essential as emotional understanding. The more we grasp our own perspective, the better we can honor those who experience the world differently. In business, this entails understanding cross-cultural communication. In relationships, it involves avoiding assumptions and embracing differences with grace.

To lead across borders with emotional fluency, attunement must be our posture. This involves understanding your emotions, recognizing those of others, and navigating diverse environments with humility and curiosity. It is not about knowing everything, but about being willing to learn. It is not about abandoning who you are, but refining how you present yourself.

This is the kind of emotional capacity that transcends borders and generations. It shapes how we work, how we lead, how we love—and how we belong.

Reflection

INNER CLARITY IN A NOISY WORLD

Inner awareness is the foundation of emotional fluency—but inner clarity is what makes that awareness actionable. It's the internal alignment that helps leaders discern, decide, and respond with authenticity in uncertain times—but in a noisy, performative world, it's also one of the easiest things to lose. These prompts encourage you to slow down and reconnect with your truth.

- What patterns, narratives, or beliefs have you internalized that no longer align with the person you are evolving into?
- When do you feel most grounded in your values—and when do you feel most disconnected from them?
- How might increased inner clarity change the way you lead, relate, and respond in uncertain or unfamiliar environments?
- How does your inner clarity influence your ability to connect with others across differences—especially those with opposing values, generational experiences, or cultural identities?

You cannot change what you're unwilling to confront. Awareness is the beginning of everything.

CHAPTER 4

Emotional Regulation During Chaos

In a reality where disorder has become the norm, our ability to remain grounded amidst chaos is not only a personal responsibility but also a leadership imperative. Emotional regulation is at the core of emotional depth. In a world conditioned to reward reaction, regulation is a radical act. It defies the pressure to perform and instead centers clarity. Regulated leaders are not emotionally absent—they are emotionally anchored. They create space where others feel safe to bring their full selves, even when the world outside is unraveling. It involves transforming a reaction into a response. It entails the capacity to experience stress, anger, fear, and uncertainty without being overwhelmed by them. This skill distinguishes leaders with emotional depth from those who are emotionally reactive.

Whether you are leading a team, raising a family, guiding a classroom, or navigating systems in crisis, your ability to practice emotional agility under pressure becomes your anchor. This is more than regulation—it's the capacity to adapt emotionally without losing your grounding. Emotional agility enables you to remain present, compassionate, and clear-minded when the world around you is not. The reality is this: Chaos will not wait for your readiness. But with emotional agility, you can meet it with both flexibility and resolve—equipped with the internal tools to steady yourself in the storm.

The Neuroscience of Emotional Hijacking

To understand emotional regulation, we must first grasp what occurs when we lose it. The brain's internal alarm system, the amygdala, helps explain why we sometimes react in ways we later regret. It inundates the body with stress hormones like adrenaline and cortisol. This automatic process, known as an amygdala hijack, clarifies why we sometimes say or do things in the heat of the moment that we later come to regret.

In this hijacked state, logic and empathy become unreachable. The brain shifts into survival mode: fight, flight, freeze, or fawn. Our capacity for critical thinking, clear communication, and effective leadership is compromised.

Regulation starts by activating the brain's prefrontal cortex, the area responsible for decision-making and emotional balance. It is in this space—between stimulus and response—that leadership is developed.

In the real world, we see this shift when leaders replace reaction with reflection—when they choose clarity over chaos. Consider the following story from a healthcare setting:

The Burnout That Sparked a Listening Circle

A hospital director noticed rising tension and turnover among nurses during the post-pandemic recovery. When she paused her standard debrief meetings and instead introduced fifteen-minute "listening circles" at shift changes, something shifted. Staff were invited to share one emotion they were carrying in—a simple act, no solutions required. Over time, morale improved. Mistakes dropped. Emotional transparency began to heal what protocols could not.

Her Mosaic Intelligence in action:

Emotional Integrity: She led with her own vulnerability first.

Cultural Flexibility: She created a rhythm that honored both Western and collectivist caregiving traditions.

Identity Agility: She showed up not just as a director, but as a witness to human pain.

Guiding Through Overwhelm: Emotional Integrity in Motion

Today's leaders carry more than performance metrics. They are charged with modeling resilience, nurturing psychological safety, and navigating an internal terrain shaped by fear, fatigue, and uncertainty.

When left unchecked, internal unrest in positions of influence often shows up in familiar patterns: micromanagement, avoidance, overwork.

Unregulated anger often disguises itself as sarcasm, blame, or withdrawal. Over time, these stress responses calcify into burnout, detachment, or emotional numbness.

But resilient professionals cultivate something different: emotional stamina.

They learn to recover without retreating. They practice the art of pausing, reflecting, and aligning—choosing discernment over reaction, even in moments that threaten to undo them.

This is not performative calm.

It is the discipline of self-regulation—a survival strategy in a world of mounting complexity.

These reactive patterns are human. But they are unsustainable.

Those rooted in emotional fluency do not suppress their emotions—they recognize them, integrate them, and lead from grounded wisdom. Their presence doesn't deny reality; it holds it. It softens chaos into calm. It replaces coercion with clarity. It shapes atmospheres through steadiness, not control.

This is not just effective leadership.

It is human-centered influence—anchored in emotional integrity.

Transforming Emotional Chaos into Emotional Tools

Emotional regulation is not about eliminating emotion; it is about learning to engage with emotions skillfully. This form of self-regulation becomes the scaffolding of emotional resilience—allowing us to remain anchored in moments when others unravel, particularly when they matter most. What follows is not a checklist, but a collection of intentional practices—a toolkit for returning to your center when the world around you feels unsteady. These tools are based on science, accessible to everyone, and transformative when used consistently.

Identify the Emotion

The first practice is to name what you feel. Neuroscience tells us that by identifying your emotion—"I feel anxious," "I feel overwhelmed"—you reduce the brain's stress response. This process is known as affect labeling. By naming the emotion, you shift from a reactive emotional state to cognitive processing. In high-stakes environments, simply acknowledging your internal state brings clarity and reduces escalation.

Box Breathing

This technique—employed by elite performers and trauma therapists—involves inhaling for four counts, holding for four, exhaling for four, and holding again. It activates the parasympathetic nervous system and induces calm in the body. Before a meeting or conversation, just three rounds can restore groundedness and focus.

The Ninety-Second Rule

Neuroscientist Dr. Jill Bolte Taylor teaches that an emotion's chemical presence in the body lasts for about ninety seconds. After that, we maintain the emotion through our thoughts. When you feel triggered, take a moment of ninety seconds before responding. Allow your body to settle. Then ask yourself, "What story am I telling myself right now?" This pause can mean the difference between reacting and regretting.

Reframing

Cognitive reframing enables you to reinterpret a situation with clarity and purpose. Rather than thinking, "My team is underperforming," a leader might reframe the moment as, "My team may need additional direction or support." This shift transforms frustration into opportunity.

Emotional Journaling

Writing serves as a powerful tool for emotional integration. Taking five minutes each day to reflect on challenges, the emotions that arose, and what you wish to carry forward encourages release, understanding, and direction.

Grounded in Values

In difficult moments, returning to our core values grounds us. When emotions rise, ask yourself, "What do I want to embody right now?" Let your answer align with your values—courage, grace, and integrity. This exemplifies anchored leadership. Values act as emotional stabilizers.

From Reactivity to Emotionally Anchored Leadership

Emotionally reactive leaders act on impulse and erode trust. In contrast, emotionally anchored leaders respond with thoughtfulness, model steadiness, and cultivate environments where people feel safe to bring their full selves forward.

They do not suppress their emotions—they examine them. They create safety for others while maintaining boundaries for themselves. And they model recovery, showing that stress can be metabolized—not simply endured.

The Generational Influence of Regulated Leadership

Older generations were taught to suppress emotion in the name of professionalism. Younger generations, encouraged to express themselves more freely, are often navigating without the tools to regulate what they feel.

Attuned guidance bridges the generational gap.

It validates emotion without letting it become destructive.

It teaches that emotional presence is not indulgent—it's a form of accountability.

And that regulation is not repression—it's relational integrity in motion.

Leaders who regulate emotions influence not only the workplace but also homes and communities. Their presence serves as a steadying force—not because they are unshaken, but because they have learned how to anchor themselves.

Emotional Containment versus Suppression

Regulation is not repression. Suppression avoids; regulation engages. It is the difference between ignoring pain and utilizing it as data. Unchecked anger transforms into aggression. Unprocessed fear leads to avoidance. However, when engaged wisely, emotions become sources of clarity. Suppression is like sealing steam in a pressure cooker without a release valve—it builds until something breaks. Containment, on the other hand, is like placing that steam in a well-designed engine—it fuels momentum, direction, and control. One leads to rupture; the other to forward movement.

Insights Gained from a Car Accident

One evening in Manhattan, I watched from a restaurant window as a driver backed into my parked car. Instinct kicked in—adrenaline, defensiveness, frustration. I rushed outside, bracing for conflict. But what I encountered surprised me.

He remained calm. He stepped out, acknowledged his mistake, and handed me his insurance without hesitation. His voice was steady and low, his presence grounded. He didn't match my intensity—he neutralized it. And as he did, the storm inside me began to settle.

There were no raised voices. No drama. Just clarity and calm. Because he stayed composed, I did too. We resolved everything quickly and respectfully.

What stayed with me wasn't the damage—insurance handled that easily. It was his energy. His calmness influenced mine. It reminded me that peace is not passivity; it's leadership.

Not every situation unfolds gracefully. But this one did—because someone chose not to meet intensity with more intensity. He brought calm into the moment, and I followed.

That moment taught me this: Your energy enters a room before your words do. When you learn to regulate—not suppress—your emotional state, you create space for restoration instead of destruction.

Grounded awareness is not weakness. It is strength without force. It's authority that doesn't shout. His presence showed me that emotional regulation isn't shrinking—it's the courage to lead when tension calls for control.

Calm Is Contagious

Your energy arrives before your words. When you enter a room with composure, you allow others to exhale. Regulated leaders create emotional containers in which others feel safe. They exemplify self-mastery without ego. They embody peace, not to be passive, but to foster truth, healing, and restoration.

Chaos is inevitable, but it doesn't have to define you. Allow emotional literacy to steady you, and let your calm become the calm that others remember.

Reflection

EMOTIONAL REGULATION DURING CHAOS

Regulating emotions in calm conditions is one thing—doing so under pressure is where real growth begins. These prompts help you uncover what lies beneath your reactivity and how to lead from emotional clarity, not control.

- What emotion do you most often suppress under stress—and what might it be trying to teach you?
- When was the last time someone else's calm helped regulate your own? What stood out about their presence?
- How might your leadership shift if you responded to chaos not with control, but with clarity?
- How might your self-regulation model emotional safety for individuals from marginalized or underrepresented communities?

Your greatest strength in chaos is not control—it's emotional clarity anchored in emotional availability.

CHAPTER 5

Resilience Through Motivation

Motivation is often perceived as an advantage in stable times. However, during periods of profound change, it becomes a lifeline—an essential force that can either strengthen or shatter a team's spirit.

We all strive to be productive in a world that demands more from us than ever—more output, greater speed, and relentless endurance. We are expected to keep moving while grieving, adapt while still processing, and perform while barely hanging on. In such conditions, motivation can start to feel hollow—a buzzword, a burden, a myth.

Yet, amid the chaos, true motivation—rooted in purpose, meaning, and identity—is not about pushing harder. It is about anchoring deeper. It is not about forcing productivity but about remembering why you are still standing.

Resilience isn't just about bouncing back; it's about building forward. Motivation serves as the fuel that makes this possible—not superficial inspiration, but inner clarity rooted in resilience. It declares, "I know who I am, and I understand why I am still here."

Pressure Cooker: Life on the Edge

Let's be honest—many of us are operating at the edge of our emotional capacity.

From a management perspective, this manifests as disengagement, increasing burnout, and high turnover. On a personal level, it feels like constant change with no time to catch your breath. You are expected to trend upward, even as your spirit yearns to slow down.

In many high-pressure environments, resilience is often misdefined as relentlessness. However, being driven is not the same as being grounded. One is frequently fueled by ego and external validation, while the other stems from inner alignment and purpose.

When people are asked to do too much for too long, motivation turns mechanical. They start to question, "What's the point? Why does this even matter? Am I just surviving—or actually living?" These questions are not signs of laziness or weakness; they are indications of misalignment, and misalignment is the enemy of motivation.

Burnout is not a reflection of your capacity—it is often a reflection of prolonged misalignment. When your values are buried beneath urgency, or your time is filled with what depletes rather than nourishes, the spirit begins to stall. Reframing burnout not as a failure, but as a signal, invites you to recalibrate rather than retreat.

When purpose is present—even in the face of pain—motivation becomes intrinsic. And intrinsic motivation is the type that lasts. Extrinsic motivation is like a spark—it flares when recognition, deadlines, or rewards are present, but quickly fades. Intrinsic motivation, however, is more like a pilot light. It burns quietly beneath the surface, fed by purpose, values, and meaning. When everything else fails, it's the pilot light that keeps the flame alive.

Motivation in Adversity: Discovering Significance in the Flames

Adversity possesses the power to break or build you. The difference lies in your beliefs about the experience. Psychologist

Viktor Frankl, a Holocaust survivor and author of *Man's Search for Meaning*, stated that people can endure almost any "how" if they have a strong enough "why." His words represent more than theory—they serve as a blueprint for sustaining motivation in times of hardship.

In leadership, we often speak about vision. However, in times of adversity, it's not vision that sustains us—it's the conviction that what we are doing and enduring matters beyond the moment. Meaning does not erase struggle; it redeems it.

Whether you are navigating a crisis, recovering from a loss, or undergoing personal transformation, the key to staying motivated is to connect pain to purpose. That connection turns obstacles into stepping stones and struggle into strength.

Leadership and Management: System-Level Motivation

Resilience anchored in purpose cannot be assumed; it must be intentionally cultivated within the organizational culture. Leaders who pursue performance without emotional harmony often foster burnout. Teams do not only need direction—they need meaningful direction. They must understand why their work matters, how their contributions fit into a larger mission, and that their well-being is as important as the bottom line.

This is where emotionally attuned leadership becomes indispensable. Today's managers are not simply task assigners—they are curators of meaning. They help individuals reconnect with purpose, especially in times of change, uncertainty, and transition.

A 2022 McKinsey report found that employees who find purpose in their work are four times more engaged and five times more likely to stay long-term. Yet, many organizations still expect individuals to arrive already inspired, rather than creating environments that foster inspiration.

Motivation does not thrive on demand; it must be nurtured through intentional modeling, positive reinforcement, and systems that foster clarity, support, and alignment.

Motivation as Individual Evolution

Resilience fueled by inner purpose is not just about perseverance—it is about alignment. Change does more than disrupt routines; it reshapes identity. As industries evolve and personal landscapes shift, you are invited to grow—not reactively, but intentionally. Growth asks you to release what once defined you—titles, habits, roles, or expectations that no longer reflect who you are today. In these moments, motivation is not a burst of energy—it is a steady internal force, guiding you through discomfort and toward clarity.

It keeps you grounded when the world outside feels uncertain. It fuels your steps—not because others are watching, but because your purpose transcends your circumstances.

Consider: What am I discovering about myself during this period of pressure? Who am I evolving into through this process of adaptation? What would I stand up for—even if no one cheered?

Purpose in Practice: Daily Anchors to Build Resilience

Motivation is not always a roar; sometimes, it's a whisper that says, "Take one more step." In times of rapid change, motivation can feel fleeting. However, sustainable motivation is not rooted in emotion—it's anchored in purpose.

To stay resilient, we must transition from a mood-based approach to a mindset-based way of living. Daily practices like meditation, journaling, and intention-setting are not luxuries; they are vital lifelines.

Reconnect with Your Why

Clarity of purpose is one of our greatest sources of strength. When we lose touch with our deeper reasons, our motivation begins to wane.

Ask yourself: Who does this serve? What impact does this create? What legacy am I building?

Write it down. Speak it out loud. Let it guide you.

Reclaim Your Wins

Hardship can create amnesia. We forget what we have already overcome.

Keep a journal of small victories. They are not just records of progress; they are reminders of your resilience.

Break the Day into Chapters

Overwhelm robs us of momentum. Divide the day into smaller parts—chapters. Set micro-goals. Recognize completion. Reset.

This rhythm fosters sustainable energy. And it begins with inner clarity—the grounded awareness that distinguishes urgency from importance, noise from truth, and pressure from purpose. And it begins with inner clarity—a grounded awareness that helps you separate urgency from importance and noise from truth.

Connect to a Greater Narrative

When motivation wanes, meaning should fill the gap. Serve others. Listen. Encourage. Acts of service remind us that we are part of something larger.

Visualize Forward

Ask yourself: What future version of me would express gratitude for my actions today?

Let that answer guide your next step—not from pressure, but from purpose.

When Motivation Feels Like a Mirage

There will be days when motivation feels out of reach. Grant yourself grace. You are not required to produce endless energy—you are encouraged to remain grounded in what truly matters.

Motivation may not always be consistent, but commitment can be. When driven by purpose, commitment transforms into a quiet yet powerful force.

Legacy Leadership: Inspiring Beyond the Moment

Legacy is not built in comfort; it is forged in tension—when you continue to show up not for applause, but because that is your true self.

Whether you lead a team, classroom, business, or household, your motivation influences more than just your output. It impacts culture, connection, and emotional safety.

Lessons on Motivation: A Two-Way Street

Organizations often expect individuals to be self-motivated—solution-oriented, proactive, and internally driven. While some people naturally develop that mindset, here's the tension: not everyone begins there, and not every system supports it.

In many workplaces, motivation is often thought to arise solely from compensation. However, research challenges this perspective. A 2022 Gallup poll revealed that only twenty-one percent of employees worldwide are engaged at work, despite receiving fair pay. A McKinsey study discovered that seventy percent of employees find purpose more in the work itself and the environment than in their salaries.

Motivation is not solely about money; it encompasses meaning as well. We are currently living through a time of profound disruption—economically, socially, and emotionally. Everyone requires motivation, leaders included. However, in today's workplace, motivation is no longer a one-way flow; it is relational.

Leaders seek energy, responsiveness, and innovation from their teams. In turn, teams seek clarity, care, and connection from their leaders. Motivation is no longer hierarchical—it is mutual. When this energy is reciprocal, performance becomes sustainable.

Organizations rooted in emotional fluency understand that motivation is cultivated, not coerced. They foster encouragement as a rhythm, not a reaction. And they invest in purpose and safety as conditions for sustained engagement.

In return, they receive more than mere compliance. They gain creativity, collaboration, commitment, and resilience.

So, whether you lead a team or contribute to one, keep this in mind:

Motivation involves more than individual willpower.

It encompasses collective energy.

It is about cultivating environments where people are inspired to give their best—not only for what they do, but also for who they are.

Motivation at its highest level is not just about performance—it's about legacy. It asks, "What will endure because I chose not to give up?" The most resilient leaders are not fueled by applause, but by alignment. They are guided by a vision greater than the moment and anchored in a purpose that time cannot erase.

> ## Reflection

RESILIENCE THROUGH MOTIVATION

True motivation doesn't always roar. Sometimes, it whispers in the quiet after disappointment or reemerges in the midst of burnout. These prompts invite you to hold space for the deeper motivations that persist even when external rewards or validation fade. Let them guide you inward—toward what fuels you when nothing else seems to ignite.

- What keeps you grounded when external motivation fades—and how often do you return to it?
- When has adversity helped you uncover a deeper purpose or clarity of self?
- In what ways could you create (or ask for) a more motivating environment—one that reflects both your values and your emotional needs?
- In what ways can aligning your motivation with inclusive impact help sustain resilience—not just for yourself, but for others who look to you for guidance?

Resilience is not about pushing harder. It's about staying connected to what matters most—especially when it would be easier to give up.

A Return to the Self

You have carried so much for so long.
Not everything you carry belongs to you.
This serves as your permission to let it go.

Returning to stillness. Trusting your body's wisdom.
Hearing your own voice again.
Healing starts with awareness.
Awareness starts with breath.
Return to your true self.

PART II

LEADING WITH EMOTIONAL INTEGRITY

––––– ✦✦✦✦✦ –––––

Leadership today requires more than authority—it demands emotional alignment. This section examines how empathy, trust, and relational clarity shape powerful leadership in divided, high-stakes environments. Emotional integrity becomes not only a personal standard but also a cultural force.

CHAPTER 6

The Return to Empathy

The Rhythm of Empathy

If emotional literacy has a heartbeat, its rhythm is empathy. It is not merely a soft skill—it is a sustaining force. Empathy bridges difference, builds trust, and repairs what disruption has fractured. Without it, we become efficient but cold, visible but unseen, connected yet indifferent.

Earlier in this book, we named the slow erosion of empathy in modern life. But this chapter is not a repetition—it is a return. Not a nostalgic longing for how things were, but a deeper journey forward. It is an invitation to reimagine what empathy can become when we treat it not as a sentiment, but as a practice.

The Quiet Cost of Disconnection

I once coached a senior executive who had built a wildly successful company, yet couldn't understand why his team avoided him. "I'm always fair," he told me. And he was. But fairness without warmth, correction without connection, had created an emotional drought. His team complied—but they no longer cared. What he hadn't realized was that empathy is not optional in leadership. Without it, performance may continue—but people disengage. Influence becomes transactional. Trust dissolves.

In every domain—education, healthcare, business, family—this quiet loss of empathy is felt. We witness lives that function but don't flourish. Conversations that transact information without exchange of presence. Leadership that directs without ever really seeing. People are showing up, but not feeling seen. This is the cost of emotional disconnection—not always visible, but always consequential.

Rebuilding the Muscle of Empathy

Empathy is not a fixed quality. It is not something we either have or don't. It is more like a muscle: it grows stronger with use and weakens with neglect. And today, many of us are moving through the world relationally atrophied. Chronic stress, fear, division, and digital fatigue all diminish our ability to attune to others. But neuroscience gives us hope. Emotional attunement, as Dr. Richard Davidson notes, stimulates parts of the brain responsible for compassion and self-regulation. The more we practice empathy, the more naturally and deeply it becomes part of who we are. The opposite is also true. Left unpracticed, empathy doesn't just fade—it calcifies.

Rebuilding empathy begins in the small, intentional moments. When we slow down and ask what someone is really trying to express. When we resist the urge to fix and instead say, "That makes sense. I'm here." When we listen—not for our turn to speak, but for understanding. These acts, though simple, are radical in a world that moves fast and feels shallow.

Empathy Across Generations

It helps to understand that empathy wears different faces across generations. Baby Boomers often demonstrate care through loyalty and quiet service. Generation X brings empathy through dependability and practical problem-solving. Millennials have embraced emotional vocabulary and value transparency, but often carry exhaustion from emotional overextension. Generation Z is expressive, courageous in naming injustice, and deeply invested in authenticity—but still navigating how to regulate their emotional openness.

No one expression is more valid than another, but these generational nuances often go unacknowledged, and when misunderstood, they can deepen division. What looks like coldness may be quiet care. What seems like oversharing may be a cry for connection. Relational fluency means learning to read beyond our default interpretations.

From Individuals to Systems

Of course, empathy must live beyond individuals—it must be embedded into our systems. Without systemic support, relational wisdom remains an isolated trait rather than a cultural norm. In schools, emotional fluency should be woven into how we manage classrooms, support teachers, and design curriculum. In organizations, it must influence how we give feedback, navigate conflict, and measure success. In families, empathy needs to shape discipline, communication, and modeling. Emotional safety becomes sustainable only when it becomes structural.

What Empathy Is—And Isn't

Empathy, however, is not about agreement. Nor is it emotional absorption. Real empathy makes room for two truths: I can honor your experience and still remain grounded in my own. Empathy does not require collapsing our boundaries. It asks us to widen our presence. It is not about taking on someone else's pain—it is about staying close to it without retreating or rushing past it. That is the discipline. That is the power.

Relearning Empathy: Practical Tools

If you feel emotionally distant or uncertain about how to reconnect, you are not alone. Empathy can be revived. The following practices are not exhaustive, but they serve as a starting point.

Slow Down to See People

In every interaction, take a moment to ask, "What is this person really trying to express?" Beneath the words, what emotions are emerging? Emotional availability fosters emotional space.

Practice Mirror Listening

Reflect back what you hear: "It seems like you are feeling frustrated because you feel unheard. Is that correct?" This approach not only clarifies but also builds trust.

Ask Better Questions

Move beyond asking, "How are you?" Instead, try phrases like, "What has been heavy for you lately?" or "What do you wish people understood about what you are carrying?" Deep questions encourage deeper connections.

Honor Emotions Without Fixing

Respond with, "That makes sense. That is really hard. I'm here for you." Most people are not looking for answers—they need to be seen.

Expand Your Emotional Imagination

Read stories, watch films, and engage in conversations that challenge your assumptions. Exposure expands your ability to attune. It deepens your emotional fluency and strengthens your capacity to see the world through someone else's lens.

Embedding Relational Intelligence into Systems

For emotional presence to thrive, it must be embedded in systems—not merely demonstrated by individuals. In schools, this means weaving relational intelligence into classroom management, curriculum design, and teacher development. In organizations, it should shape leadership styles, feedback models, and wellness strategies. In families, emotional literacy must show up in discipline, communication, and example.

Emotional safety is sustainable when it is systemic.

The Emotional Return: Healing What Was Fragmented

We are not returning to how things were. We are returning to what has always mattered.

The point is not to go backward, but to move inward—to slow down, to notice again, to care more deeply. In a world that pushes us to perform, produce, and protect our image, empathy invites something quieter and more radical: to be fully human in the presence of another.

The return to empathy is not sentimental. It is strategic. It is what allows teams to rebuild trust after rupture. It is what helps students feel safe enough to speak. It is what turns correction into connection, and what transforms difference from a threat into an opportunity.

Empathy is not weakness. It is the discipline of holding space in a world that rushes to fill it. It is the strength to stay grounded when others escalate. It is the wisdom to connect before you correct, and the maturity to understand before you react. Empathy is not about control—it's about presence. And presence, when practiced consistently, heals what fragmentation has severed.

Lessons from Saudi Arabia: Emotional Fluency Across Borders

Serving as a professor and internal auditor at a university in Al Khobar, Saudi Arabia, offered one of the most humbling and expansive experiences of emotional fluency I've ever encountered. As a Western educator supporting both students and faculty, I entered a space where technical expertise was necessary—but not sufficient. What the environment truly demanded was emotional agility: the capacity to observe, adapt, and make room for cultural complexity without compromising authenticity.

The faculty was profoundly international. I collaborated with colleagues from India, Pakistan, South Africa, Nigeria, Zimbabwe, Egypt, Jordan, Lebanon, Sudan, Canada, the United States, and across Europe. Together, we held the shared responsibility of delivering an education that honored both academic rigor and cultural nuance.

This diversity showed up not just in language or background—but in how we approached teaching, learning, communication, and time. Some colleagues thrived in structure and precision. Others led with fluidity and relationships. The students reflected the same mosaic—some gravitated toward direct instruction, while others came from traditions where listening held more weight than questioning.

Emotional fluency became essential—not only in how I engaged others, but in how I examined myself. I had to unlearn many Western assumptions about what "effective" teaching looked like. I had to slow down—not because students lacked capability, but because learning was relational. Mutual respect held more weight than pace. I began to understand that silence could mean reverence, not disengagement. That disagreement was best offered in private, not in public. That feedback had to preserve dignity in order to foster trust.

In that context, emotional presence wasn't soft. It was strategic. Deliberate. Intelligent. It acted as a translator across cultures, time zones, and worldviews. The faculty room became its own kind of global classroom. Every conversation was a quiet lesson in relational intelligence. We exchanged not only lesson plans, but values, beliefs, and lived truths.

That season taught me that this work is not about being agreeable—it's about being attuned. It is the ability to read emotional tone, honor cultural nuance, and remain aware of your own impact. Saudi Arabia didn't merely ask me to teach—it invited me to evolve. In that invitation, emotional fluency became both the path and the destination.

Reflection

THE RETURN TO ATTUNEMENT

In a world of fast takes and filtered interactions, slowing down becomes a radical act of connection. These questions invite you to step out of performance, assumption, and comfort—and into something more human, more aware, and more lasting.

- Where in your life or leadership have assumptions replaced curiosity—and how might you shift that dynamic?
- What form of emotional fluency are you being called to practice: listening, groundedness, boundaries, or compassionate presence?
- How have your experiences with difference or discomfort shaped your understanding of connection?
- In what ways have you created emotionally safe environments for voices that differ from your own?
- How does your ability to self-regulate impact your inclusive leadership presence?

Emotional attunement is not agreement—it is the willingness to see, stay, and soften when it matters most.

CHAPTER 7

Inclusive Social Skills for Divided Times

In an age marked by disconnection, rising tension, and emotional fatigue, one of the most essential forms of intelligence we can cultivate is the ability to connect—especially across divides.

Social skills are often dismissed as charm or conversational ease, but in emotionally attuned leadership, they become something far more consequential. They serve as the connective tissue between people who disagree, as the steady hand during conflict, and as the quiet power that turns discord into dialogue. They're not ornamental—they're urgent.

This chapter is not about niceties. It's about learning to navigate tension with truth, to remain present when discomfort arrives, and to build trust in places that have forgotten what it feels like.

The Erosion of Civil Discourse

Civil discourse has deteriorated in recent years. Once a venue for diverse perspectives and thoughtful dialogue, public conversation has become more combative and binary. It has transformed into "us versus them," "right versus wrong," and "win versus lose."

Beneath the noise often lies a silent plea: See me. Hear me. Do not dismiss me simply because I am different.

Human beings are not wired for permanent division; we are relational by nature. However, even simple conversations can feel threatening when fear, shame, or exhaustion dominate the emotional climate. This is why social skills must evolve. Communicating is no longer enough; we must connect—not just to inform, but to inspire trust, express care, and invite understanding.

Social Intelligence: The Relational Expression of Emotional Depth

Daniel Goleman, who popularized the concept of emotional intelligence, described social intelligence as emotional depth applied in a relational context. It encompasses the ability to read nonverbal cues, navigate power dynamics with humility, repair trust ruptures, and create emotionally safe environments.

These are not merely "nice-to-have" traits; they are essential for sustainable leadership and relational integrity. Whether you are leading a team, mentoring a student, raising a child, or mending a fractured relationship, social intelligence is a universal skill that enables you to lead with clarity, empathy, and grace.

Generational Tensions and the Importance of Fluent Communication

Many of today's divisions are generational. Different age groups communicate using distinct emotional languages. Older generations often prioritize respect, loyalty, and order, while younger generations tend to value authenticity, voice, and transparency.

What one group perceives as entitlement, another may interpret as empowerment. What one person sees as disrespect, another may regard as truth-telling. These differences are not failures; they are invitations to engage more deeply, decode emotional signals, and understand diverse expressions of care and conviction.

These disconnects do not signify a lack of values. Instead, they reflect various ways of expressing the same desire: to be heard, to matter, and to belong. Socially intelligent communication helps us decode these differences and uncover the common humanity beneath.

Social Fluency in Leadership and Management

Leaders today are not only accountable for results—they are also responsible for emotional ecosystems. Social fluency refers to the ability to navigate conversations, conflicts, and collaborations with emotional clarity and purpose.

Socially fluent leaders gauge the emotional tone of a room before speaking. They listen more than they talk, particularly when tensions are elevated. They differentiate between intent and impact. They create space for disagreement while upholding a shared purpose.

This fluency fosters psychological safety, a concept popularized by Harvard researcher Amy Edmondson. It refers to the belief that individuals can voice their thoughts, take risks, and engage fully without fear of humiliation. In cultures led by socially intelligent leaders, psychological safety is not merely a possibility—it is the norm.

Navigating Difficult Conversations: A Relationally Attuned Approach

Difficult conversations are not a sign of dysfunction; they are a sign of maturity. Emotionally attuned leaders approach them with curiosity rather than conviction. They ask, "What do you want me to understand about your experience?" or "What matters most in this conversation?"

They listen beyond words, guided by emotional literacy—recognizing the feeling beneath the message before offering logic.

Phrases like "That sounds painful" or "I see this matters to you" create emotional safety and invite trust.

They hold dual truths: you can disagree and still care, and you can be hurt yet remain open. They do not avoid rupture; instead, they repair it. Saying, "I realize I hurt you. That was not my intent, but I take responsibility," opens the door to healing and growth.

The Importance of Emotional Safety in Divided Spaces

Fostering emotional safety is one of the greatest gifts a leader can offer. It enables people to present themselves authentically, free from the fear of shame or rejection. This does not mean evading truth or accountability. It means presenting truth with compassion, establishing boundaries with dignity, and challenging behavior without dehumanizing the individual. Creating an emotionally secure environment fosters maturity and becomes a catalyst for growth.

From Social Skills to Social Healing

This chapter is not only about communication; it also emphasizes restoration. What is broken in our society cannot be healed solely through information. It will be healed through relationships—through tone, timing, and tenderness. If we listened to understand rather than to win, paused before making assumptions, named our emotions without shame, and chose to repair instead of retreating, we would create a ripple of healing.

Your Voice Is a Bridge

You don't have to fix the world. However, you can change the tone in a single room, meeting, or conversation. When grounded in empathy, authenticity, and discipline, your voice serves as a bridge. It disarms defensiveness, opens hearts, and invites others to reconnect with their shared humanity. This isn't idealism; it's emotional leadership in action, and it's needed now more than ever.

Building Inclusive Communication Across Emotional and Cultural Divides

Inclusive communication is more than being kind—it is the ability to hold emotional space for difference, discomfort, and complexity without shutting down.

Leaders who practice inclusive communication listen beyond agreement. They ask questions not to debate, but to understand. They speak with the intention of connecting, not convincing.

This form of communication requires cultural curiosity, emotional flexibility, and the willingness to be wrong without becoming defensive. It asks us to slow down—not to censor ourselves, but to become more attuned to how our presence, tone, and language impact others.

It also means making space for voices that are not always heard. In emotionally safe environments, people don't just speak—they risk being fully themselves. That risk becomes a gift when leaders demonstrate emotional fluency and model accountability.

Lessons from Athletics: The Impact of Silent Support

Long before I became a consultant, professor, or trainer, I was an athlete. The lessons I learned on the track, in the gym, and through rigorous practices continue to shape my leadership today.

Athletics, at its core, is a language—and much of it is nonverbal. A glance. A gesture. A steadying presence. One of my earliest lessons came during a cross-country training session. I was hitting a mental wall during the final stretch of a run. Without a word, a teammate—sensing I needed support—came alongside me. He did not coach or advise. He simply ran. His authenticity conveyed what words could not.

I remember another race just as clearly. I was physically prepared but emotionally drained. A fellow runner—not a teammate, but an opponent—noticed my internal struggle. Instead of passing me or leaving me behind, she slowed her pace and ran beside me. She never spoke; she simply stayed. We crossed the finish line together and hugged. I do not remember her face or name, but I remember the solidarity.

That moment taught me that winning isn't always about crossing the finish line first. Sometimes, it's about finishing strong—and not finishing alone.

Athletics has always mirrored life. Now more than ever, athletes are called to lead not only with physical strength but also with emotional maturity. They navigate adversity, manage pressure, and shape team cultures in increasingly diverse and high-stakes environments.

Emotional depth enhances performance through character. It aids athletes in coping with disappointment, forging connections, and staying grounded. It encourages them to lead with empathy, not solely with strength.

While athletics was the first place I encountered this kind of support, it would not be the last. I would see it again—in boardrooms, meetings, and moments of organizational pressure.

From Track to Table: Leadership and the Power of Quiet Support

I sat in a high-level leadership meeting. The numbers were down, and tension filled the room. Leaders from various departments had gathered, each bearing the burden of missed targets, equipment issues, and escalating expectations. Eyes scanned the room, and the unspoken question lingered: Who would take the fall?

Instead of deflecting or assigning blame, a senior leader stepped forward. He acknowledged the challenge without placing any accusations. He bore the weight of the moment with quiet strength.

Then something unexpected happened. When the pressure shifted toward one team member, no one stepped back. No one distanced themselves from the situation.

We leaned in, holding the tension together and sharing the silence. We absorbed the weight as a team—not through explanation or defense, but through shared steadiness.

In that moment, I recognized a familiar kind of emotional fluency—one I had first cultivated as an athlete. It was the unspoken support, the intuitive ability to read the room, and the wisdom to know when to speak and when to simply stand beside someone. It was the quiet power of understanding that "we" will always carry more strength than "me."

In business, leadership, and life, social intelligence is not always loud. It does not seek recognition. Yet, it is present—in how we show up under pressure, how we protect one another when the stakes are high, and how we hold space when retreat would be easier.

That meeting reminded me of a lesson I learned long before I entered corporate spaces: leadership is not about being the loudest voice in the room; it is about maintaining groundedness under pressure and having the courage to hold discomfort with dignity.

The best teams—whether on the track, in the boardroom, or in the classroom—are not only efficient; they support one another. Every member is important, and every voice is acknowledged.

This is the leadership we desire—not based in ego or fear, but grounded in authenticity, humility, and trust.

INCLUSIVE SOCIAL SKILLS FOR DIVIDED TIMES

In emotionally charged environments, our social skills transcend mere tools—they become the means by which we protect, repair, or restore relationships. These prompts encourage reflection on how you show up in moments of tension and how your emotional steadiness influences the unfolding of events.

- When was the last time your steady energy—not your words—made a meaningful difference in a conversation or group dynamic?
- What emotional habits do you bring into disagreement—defensiveness, listening, withdrawal, or repair?
- Where in your leadership or relationships could you replace explanation with grounded connection, or correction with care?
- What inclusive communication habits can you begin to build that create belonging across emotional, cultural, and ideological divides?

In divided times, how you show up matters more than what you say.

CHAPTER 8

Trust as a Leadership Practice Rooted in Inclusion

Rebuilding trust requires listening without defensiveness—especially when power, privilege, or cultural misunderstanding is involved. Rebuilding trust is not just a personal act of repair—it is a leadership practice rooted in inclusion. Inclusive leaders understand that trust is unevenly distributed across cultures, histories, and power structures. They recognize that repairing trust across lines of difference requires more than apology; it demands accountability, emotional presence, and the willingness to sit in discomfort without retreating.

Trust is the invisible currency of every relationship, organization, and society that thrives. When trust is strong, it allows us to collaborate, communicate, and grow. But when it breaks—through betrayal, disappointment, or disconnection—it leaves behind not just silence but a scar.

Trust is often the first casualty in times of division. Rebuilding it is not a performance; it is a process. It requires emotional fluency, is sustained by both individual and collective accountability, and is guided by empathy. This emphasis on accountability fosters responsibility and long-term commitment—both are essential for rebuilding and sustaining trust.

Restoring trust is not about ignoring the past. It is about embracing the power of truth-telling, creating safe spaces for healing, and prioritizing connection over control. This process empowers us to take ownership of our relationships and organizations, guiding them toward a more authentic, resilient, and hopeful future.

The Fragility and Strength of Trust

Despite its fragility, trust is remarkably resilient, offering a beacon of hope even in the most challenging circumstances.

Trust can be shattered in an instant through dishonesty, neglect, disrespect, or betrayal. Yet, under the right conditions, it can also be restored. What breaks trust is not always malice. Sometimes, it is silence. Sometimes, it is failing to show up. Sometimes, it is a misalignment left unspoken for too long.

But here is the truth: Trust does not live in words. It resides in patterns, in consistency, and in what people do when no one is watching. This understanding empowers us to rebuild trust not by proving our intentions but by changing our impact.

The Anatomy of Broken Trust

Trust fractures in several common ways. One is through a breach of integrity—when someone lies, breaks promises, or violates shared values. Another is emotional betrayal, which can occur when someone fails to show up in a moment of need, dismisses your feelings, or minimizes your pain.

Cultural disconnection can also erode trust, particularly when identity, lived experiences, or personal perspectives are dismissed or invalidated. And finally, there is power misuse—when someone, intentionally or unintentionally, uses their position to harm, silence, or manipulate others.

These fractures are not always explosive. Sometimes, they accumulate quietly, in the form of small, repeated micro-betrayals that compound over time. But whether the break is sudden or subtle, the result is the same: relational safety collapses.

Where safety is compromised, connection cannot flourish. This highlights the crucial role of trust in forming meaningful connections.

What Enables the Repair of Trust

Emotional presence, a reliable roadmap for healing, plays a crucial role in rebuilding trust. It highlights five essential elements in the process: empathy, accountability, consistency, transparency, and time.

Empathy, the cornerstone of trust repair, is the ability to understand and share the feelings of another. It is not about rushing the process or dismissing the pain. It is about acknowledging the hurt, sitting with discomfort, and showing genuine care. Empathy says, "I understand this hurts you, and I'm willing to sit with your pain, even if it makes me uncomfortable."

Equally important is accountability. This goes beyond saying, "I'm sorry you feel that way," which often deflects responsibility. True accountability sounds like, "I see where I fell short of your expectations," or "I take full responsibility," followed by, "Here's what I'm doing to make it right." No excuses. No blame-shifting. Just ownership.

Consistency is also vital. One good conversation does not rebuild trust—sustained, reliable behavior does. Trust is restored moment by moment through follow-through, dependability, and actions aligned with words. Consistency says, "You can relax now. I'm growing into someone you can trust again."

Transparency is equally essential. Mistrust thrives in confusion. When people are unclear about your stance, they often assume the worst. Rebuilding trust requires being honest about intentions, decisions, and boundaries—even when it is uncomfortable. Transparency is not simply about sharing; it is about communicating with clarity and purpose. It keeps others informed and involved in the process of trust repair.

Finally, trust takes time. Repairing it is not a quick fix but a gradual process—especially when the wound runs deep. Emotionally attuned individuals honor the pace of healing. They do not rush forgiveness or demand immediate resolution. They understand that trust, once broken, must be rebuilt with care, patience, and consistent effort.

Here's what that kind of trust repair can look like in action:

Vignette: A Shift in Feedback Culture
A department leader noticed that feedback meetings with junior team members of color often ended in silence. One brave employee eventually spoke up, explaining that previous sessions felt more punitive than developmental.

Rather than defend her process, the leader chose to listen, express gratitude for the honesty, and co-create a new feedback rhythm grounded in safety and growth. Over time, the team began speaking more openly—and trusting more deeply. Not because mistakes disappeared, but because psychological safety was restored.

Rebuilding Trust in Leadership and Teams

In organizational life, trust is often broken in ways leaders may not immediately recognize. It can fracture through silence during a crisis, unaddressed conflict among team members, or policies that feel inequitable—such as a promotion process that appears biased or a dress code that erases cultural identity. Sometimes, it's simply the gap between what leaders say—like "We care"—and what they actually do.

Leaders grounded in emotional fluency rebuild trust not through pressure, but through presence. They show emotional availability. They acknowledge missteps. They co-create solutions. And most importantly, they lead *with* their people—not merely *for* them.

A trust-restoring leader says, "I missed something important and want to make it right." They say, "Let's rebuild this together," and "Your trust matters more than my ego."

Navigating Trust Gaps Across Cultures and Generations

Trust often breaks across cultural and generational lines. In some cultures, speaking truth to power is discouraged, which makes silence a survival mechanism. In others, direct feedback is expected, and silence can feel like a betrayal. Older generations may equate loyalty with enduring conflict quietly, while younger generations may view loyalty as the expression of truth, even at the expense of harmony.

When we fail to understand these differences, we misread intent and miss the opportunity for repair. Rebuilding trust across differences requires cultural humility, the ability to recognize our blind spots, challenge assumptions, and remain open to uncomfortable feedback. Cultural humility involves actively seeking to understand and respect the perspectives of others, even when they differ from our own. This kind of humility does not diminish our leadership; it deepens our capacity to lead with authenticity and respect.

Personal Trust Recovery: Healing After Betrayal

If you are struggling to trust again, know this: your hesitation is not a flaw. It is your nervous system trying to protect you. But protection is not the same as peace. You cannot rush into trust, but you can begin to explore it again.

Ask yourself what rebuilding trust might look like for you. Consider what boundaries you need to establish to feel safe. Engage in deep personal reflection on whether you are open to rebuilding or still grieving what was lost. Trusting again does not mean forgetting. It means believing in the possibility of something different.

Sometimes, rebuilding trust means giving someone another chance. Other times, it means rebuilding trust in yourself—in your ability to set boundaries, choose healthy relationships, and walk away when necessary. This may involve learning to recognize and respect your own needs, setting clear expectations in your relationships, and being willing to let go of situations that no longer serve you. Both are powerful.

Restoring Trust in a Fractured Society

At a collective level, trust has eroded between institutions and the people they serve. We see this when communities no longer believe in the systems meant to protect them, when employees feel replaceable instead of valued, when citizens feel unheard, overpoliced, or underrepresented, and when youth inherit broken systems and are asked to fix them with little support.

Rebuilding institutional trust requires more than words. It demands a commitment to systemic empathy, courageous accountability, and long-term investment in justice, equity, and healing. It cannot be performative. It must be authentic. And it must begin with the relationship before repair. It says, "We failed you. We see it. We own it. We are not asking you to move on—we are asking you to move forward together."

Trust Is Sacred Work

Rebuilding trust is sacred work. It is slow, deliberate, and profoundly human. In a world quick to cancel, criticize, and sever ties, choosing to rebuild is an act of bravery. Whether you caused harm or were harmed, this journey is about becoming someone safe—for others as well as for yourself.

Emotional safety is not just a trend; it is a fundamental human need. Trust is the cornerstone that makes emotional safety possible in any relationship. Therefore, let us make a conscious choice. Choose truth. Choose presence. Choose the long path of restoration. More than words—it's a commitment we make to ourselves and one another. It is how we reengage with each other and ourselves.

Lessons from Law Firms: Rebuilding Trust to Encourage Growth and Change

Trust is the true currency of influence—and once it is broken, it is difficult to earn back.

In my work consulting with law firms, I've encountered organizations that, on the surface, appeared unshakable. They had the hallmarks of success: prestige, profitability, and performance. But beneath the polished veneer, something was off. The emotional foundation had begun to crack.

Teams were fragmented. Turnover was high. The atmosphere was thick with mistrust, burnout, and quiet disengagement.

In one firm, the erosion of trust didn't happen in a single moment. It happened gradually. Cultural values had drifted out of alignment. Communication became inconsistent. Competing visions at the top created confusion below. Expectations remained sky-high, yet clarity had all but disappeared. Where innovation once thrived, complacency had crept in.

But instead of naming these shifts, people began to retreat. They went silent in meetings. Protected their roles. Focused on staying afloat rather than stepping forward. The energy changed—not all at once, but inch by inch, through a thousand small withdrawals.

Trust rarely collapses overnight.

It fractures through accumulated disappointments, broken promises, and guidance that over-directs but fails to truly connect.

I've seen it too many times: systems that reward productivity but overlook presence. Cultures that demand excellence but ignore emotional erosion. Influence built on fear or hierarchy may produce short-term results, but it cannot sustain loyalty, innovation, or wellbeing.

Trust doesn't just support culture.

It *is* the culture.

And rebuilding it requires more than strategy—it requires emotional integrity, consistent modeling, and the willingness to name what others would rather ignore.

The challenge was not only to raise performance but also to rebuild belief, to create a space where people felt safe enough to speak, be seen, and re-engage with a sense of shared purpose.

We began with three essential practices: consistency, accountability, and vulnerability.

First, we named the emotional gaps—not just operational inefficiencies, but places where people had felt dismissed or disregarded. We opened pathways for honest feedback that led to solutions, not blame. And we clarified: growth was the goal—but not at the expense of psychological safety.

One of the most powerful moments came through a realignment session. Every department was invited to share their goals, frustrations, hopes, and unspoken emotional needs. We mapped the places where vision had fragmented and rebuilt it from the inside out.

But vision alone was not enough. We also had to take team fit seriously. In environments where trust has been broken, who you bring in—or allow to stay—matters deeply. Hiring became intentional. We sought not only technical skills but also cultural alignment. We also had to release those whose attitudes or resistance to change were eroding the progress we were working hard to build.

Letting people go is never easy. But when done with clarity and compassion, it creates space for healing. It sends a clear message: this culture is no longer negotiable.

Trust did not return overnight. But it returned gradually—through leaders who followed through, systems that supported people, not just productivity, and a tone of leadership that modeled integrity rather than demanded flawlessness.

If culture eats strategy for breakfast, then trust is what fuels the appetite for change.

When trust is restored—not blindly but intentionally—it becomes the foundation for retention and renewal. It becomes the reason people stay, grow, and lead from within.

Reflection

REBUILDING TRUST ACROSS DIFFERENCES

Trust is not rebuilt through perfection; it is rebuilt through consistency. In a world shaped by division and repair, these prompts invite you to reflect on how you engage with trust as both an internal practice and a relational offering. Trust across difference requires more than words; it demands consistency, courage, and care.

- What does trust mean to you today, and how has your definition evolved through experience?
- Where in your leadership or life might a consistent presence speak louder than a promise?
- What boundaries or practices do you need to restore trust—with others or within yourself?
- How do you rebuild trust with someone whose worldview or identity challenges your own—and what role does emotional presence play in that process?

Rebuilding trust begins not with what you say—but with how you stay.

CHAPTER 9

Leading with Emotional Depth

Once, leadership was synonymous with authority, control, and a top-down approach.

The leader's word was law, and others followed suit. But this legacy model is gradually fading—not because it failed entirely, but because it no longer fits the emotional and cultural complexity of today's world.

A new paradigm is emerging—one that places emotional fluency, not hierarchy, at its center.

In our age of disruption, diversity, and deep emotional fatigue, influence must evolve. The standard markers of success—performance metrics and efficiency—are no longer enough. What's needed now is something more human, relational, and conscious.

Relational intelligence is no longer an optional asset—it is the cornerstone of meaningful guidance. It reflects the ability to navigate emotional dynamics with humility, communicate with nuance, and cultivate cultural sensitivity across diverse teams.

Leading with inner clarity means leading from within. Relational intelligence builds on this clarity—empowering us to lead in ways that strengthen connection, deepen trust, and honor complexity across every relationship. It involves consciously showing up with grounded awareness, managing one's emotional world, and practicing emotional integration—bringing past insights, present awareness, and future growth into alignment. This form of leadership transforms teams, systems, and the leaders themselves by attuning to the emotions of others and navigating relationships with intention, empathy, and insight.

The emotionally attuned leader begins with reflective awareness. They understand that leadership is not just about vision—it is about influence. Who you are determines how you lead. If you are reactive, your team will tread lightly. If you are calm, your team will feel at ease. If you are emotionally unavailable, your team will eventually disengage.

Your emotional energy shapes the climate more than your words ever could.

Guidance That Begins Within

Attuned guidance is not a sign of weakness—it is the embodiment of quiet courage. It requires emotional labor: the strength to self-regulate when everything inside you wants to react. It calls for empathy even when you are already overwhelmed, and the discipline to hold space for others while staying anchored in your own truth.

This form of relational presence prioritizes connection over control, even when it would be easier to retreat behind authority or policy. Those fluent in emotional presence respond differently under stress. When crisis arises, they don't retreat into silence or react from urgency—they ground themselves, foster honest dialogue, and tend to their own emotional state before managing others.

They understand that morale is not maintained by pressure, but by psychological safety. Innovation is not born of fear—it emerges through trust. These actions define emotionally attuned influence—where clarity and care are the default, not the exception.

The Internal Work Behind External Impact

Emotionally fluent influence is not a performance—it is a practice rooted in internal alignment. You cannot guide with empathy if your internal voice is harsh. You cannot co-regulate a team if you've never learned to regulate your own nervous system. You cannot hold others accountable without first becoming fluent in your blind spots.

This kind of influence is deeply reflective. It requires introspection before expression, value alignment before decision-making, and the humility to pause before reacting. It demands an emotional inventory—a courageous look inward to recognize when you are projecting, avoiding, or simply need to recalibrate.

True impact begins not with what you do, but with who you are willing to become.

When leaders model vulnerability, their teams become more open. When leaders acknowledge their own learning curves, teams become more curious. When leaders admit their mistakes, trust grows. This is emotional resonance—the power to influence others through the authenticity of your emotional presence.

Leading Across Generational and Cultural Boundaries

Instead of demanding uniformity, these leaders pursue understanding. They do not see age, culture, or background as barriers—they see them as invitations to lead with relational intelligence: the capacity to meet others with emotional clarity and cross-cultural wisdom.

They recognize generational dynamics and adjust their communication accordingly. Younger team members may value flexibility and feedback; older team members may prioritize loyalty and consistency. Leaders grounded in emotional fluency respond to both—honoring differences while cultivating unity.

Emotional Sustainability in Guiding Others

Perhaps most importantly, emotionally anchored professionals protect their energy. They recognize that sustainable influence cannot emerge from depletion. They establish boundaries with clarity, seek support without shame, normalize rest, and model what it means to lead from restoration—not resignation.

They don't just demonstrate strength—they cultivate it. Their resilience is not forged through repression but through intentional recovery. They lead with grounded awareness, emotional presence, and conscious pace.

This is not performative leadership—it is regenerative stewardship.

Redefining Guidance as a Human-Centered Practice

This is guidance redefined—not simply a role or title, but a responsibility to cultivate emotional wellness wherever your presence carries influence. Success is no longer measured solely by profit or productivity, but by trust, engagement, and the emotional integrity of those in your care.

Human-centered influence shifts the focus from control to connection. It reframes strength as sustainability and authority as relational accountability.

In a world that no longer trusts titles alone, people follow emotional steadiness more than position. They are drawn to leaders who are emotionally grounded, relationally aware, and profoundly human.

Reflection — Leading with Emotional Depth

Leadership begins with presence—not performance. In today's uncertain world, people are not seeking perfection; they are seeking resonance.

They are watching closely—not to critique, but to feel.
To feel safe.
To feel seen.
To feel something real.

Are you leading from fear—or from clarity?
Are you responding—or simply reacting?
Does your leadership reflect who you are now—not just who you were?

At the core, they are not asking for credentials. They are asking: *Can I trust your emotional world? Is your presence a space where I can grow?*

Let your leadership be a mirror of emotional safety—not just a model of success.

This is the power of emotional fluency in relational influence:

It transforms authority into authenticity, power into attunement, and position into purpose. In doing so, it doesn't just elevate your leadership—it uplifts everyone it touches.

Lessons from Network Marketing: Relationships Over Fear

One of my most transformative experiences in relational leadership came from an unexpected place: network marketing.

In that dynamic environment, I learned to influence without formal authority, build emotionally attuned teams from the ground up, and adapt quickly amid high pressure and ambiguity. These lessons became foundational to the Mosaic approach I use today—anchored in emotional presence, trust, and responsive connection.

While the industry has evolved, my experience unfolded during a formative season—defined by rapid growth, deep self-discovery, and the emergence of my voice as a relational strategist.

I had the privilege of leading a team of thousands—people from every walk of life: corporate professionals, business owners, retired athletes, emerging entrepreneurs, stay-at-home parents, recent college graduates, and passionate high schoolers.

In that setting, I learned a vital truth: effective guidance has little to do with titles or credentials—and everything to do with trust, emotional availability, and consistent connection.

What made it powerful was not uniformity, but the diversity of ambition and lived experience. Some teammates were seasoned executives. Others were just stepping into personal growth. Some had built six-figure careers. Others were juggling multiple jobs in hopes of building something better.

And yet—they all looked to me.

Not just for strategy, but for belief. Not just for answers, but for presence.

What they needed wasn't performance—it was emotional steadiness.

One story still lingers with me. A woman who recently joined the team—highly accomplished in her corporate life—came into the space not out of financial necessity but for growth. Her goals were not about replacing income; they were about rediscovering herself. One evening, she called me, feeling discouraged. The results had not yet arrived, and self-doubt was creeping in. Instead of offering her a strategy, I offered her my grounded attention. I reminded her that this journey was not about proving anything to anyone—it was about evolving into who she already sensed herself to be. She stayed. She grew. And it mattered.

At the same time, I mentored eager twenty-year-olds—sharp, coachable, and filled with potential. They carried none of the baggage of past failures and weren't constrained by old stories. Some of them soared. I watched them build momentum fueled only by belief and consistency.

It was in those moments that I witnessed the power of emotionally attuned influence in real time—how belief, when nurtured with care, can surpass experience.

This contrast—between the seasoned and the seeking—became a proving ground for my relational guidance. I learned that impactful influence is not about controlling outcomes; it's about holding space. It's not about being right—it's about being real.

In corporate spaces, I was once told, *"It's better to be feared than liked."* I still remember the sting of those words. At the time, I was guiding with emotional clarity and compassion. Rather than being celebrated, I was warned. And yes—some did exploit that kindness, just as predicted. But they missed the long game.

They overlooked the staying power of trust-centered guidance.

Years later, I can walk into rooms with those same former team members and be met with respect, gratitude, and connection—not because I demanded it, but because I *earned* it. I led with empathy, not fear. And that has become my legacy.

We have all encountered both ends of the influence spectrum. We've worked under those who controlled through fear—and those who uplifted through belief. The individuals who leave the deepest mark are not the ones who micromanage or manipulate. They're the ones who see your potential and dare to lead with heart, integrity, and presence.

Network marketing tested and refined my emotional capacity in ways I never anticipated. It sharpened my relational awareness, stretched my emotional regulation, and revealed that the most enduring form of influence comes not from performance—but from presence.

As I transitioned into consulting, executive coaching, and organizational development, the emotional depth and relational insight I gained during that chapter became one of my greatest assets.

To lead with emotional clarity is to prioritize humanity over hierarchy. It means recognizing your team not just as roles to manage, but as whole people to support, nurture, and honor.

That kind of leadership always prevails in the end.

Reflection

LEADING WITH EMOTIONAL DEPTH

Leadership is no longer about being the loudest in the room; it's about being the most emotionally anchored. These prompts invite you to reexamine not just how you lead, but who you're growing into as a leader. The emotional tone you set often matters more than any strategy you implement.

- Where in your leadership do you need more presence—and less performance?
- How does your emotional state shape the safety, tone, or trust of those you lead?
- What internal habit or mindset shift could elevate the emotional culture around you?
- What would it look like to lead with emotional depth in environments where your identity or values are not fully understood?

The most enduring leaders aren't the most polished—they're the most emotionally attuned.

CHAPTER 10

The Emotionally Attuned Leader in Crisis

Crisis reveals character. It magnifies what is already present—fear, courage, clarity, or confusion—and brings every emotional dynamic to the surface. It strips away pretense and forces decisions that can either fracture teams or forge trust. For the leader, it becomes the ultimate test—not of strategy, but of grounded steadiness.

In moments of disruption, people do not merely seek direction—they search for emotional anchors. They need leaders who stay steady in uncertainty and acknowledge the weight of the moment without being overtaken by it. This is where emotional agility becomes essential: the ability to respond flexibly without losing grounding. It is a clear, present, and deeply human form of leadership that steadies the storm.

This type of leadership cannot be performed; it must be cultivated. Crisis is not merely an event—it is a mirror. Leaders rooted in emotional fluency know how to interpret what they see reflected in that mirror—with humility, clarity, and resilience.

The Emotional Anatomy of a Crisis

When a crisis strikes—globally, organizationally, or personally—the body reacts before the mind can respond. The brain's emotional center activates, triggering a fight-or-flight response. Stress hormones surge, breathing shortens, and rational thought recedes as survival instincts take over. This is biology, not weakness.

If leaders fail to recognize this response in themselves and others, they risk growing reactive, impulsive, or emotionally disengaged. Psychologist Daniel Goleman refers to this as an "amygdala hijack." In this state, even well-intentioned leaders may revert to behaviors that foster fear instead of stability—micromanaging, avoiding, blaming, or shutting down.

Leaders grounded in emotional fluency break this pattern. They self-regulate before seeking to regulate others. They recognize that inner clarity is not optional—it is essential. Without internal grounding, they risk transmitting their anxiety to their teams instead of providing reassurance.

Leading from Within

Leadership during a crisis begins with inner clarity. Emotionally attuned leaders are aware of their own emotional state—not to suppress it, but to manage it with intention. This does not require certainty. It calls for alignment with core values while allowing space for the emotions that naturally arise.

That internal stability becomes external safety. People mirror the emotional tone of their leaders. When a leader panics, teams spiral into chaos. When a leader goes silent, teams feel abandoned. But when a leader communicates calmly, listens openly, and breathes with intention, they become a stabilizing force amid the storm.

This is not about charisma—it is about consistency. The steady calm of a self-regulated leader becomes a source of strength and trust.

Crisis Communication as Emotional Leadership

Communication in a crisis shapes not only perception but also emotional climate. Words can either calm or inflame. Emotionally anchored communication offers clarity, compassion, and composure. It does not deny reality—it speaks truth with care.

According to the *Harvard Business Review*, effective crisis communication is built on three pillars: transparency, empathy, and direction. Transparency involves acknowledging what is known and what is not. Empathy recognizes the significance of the moment. Direction offers a path forward, even if it is temporary.

Leaders who communicate this way do more than just deliver information—they convey emotion. They create a safe space for vulnerability without sacrificing hope. Their grounded energy provides reassurance. Their tone calms the room. Their honesty fosters trust.

Emotional Agility in Unpredictable Situations

Flexibility is essential during crisis. Emotionally agile leaders demonstrate the ability to stay curious, grounded, and responsive amid constant change. Psychologist Susan David defines emotional agility as the capacity to respond effectively to shifting emotions without becoming consumed by them.

Rigid authority collapses under pressure. Emotionally agile leaders respond with flexibility, presence, and clarity. They reshape roles, recalibrate priorities, and give voice to the unspoken. They honor grief, fear, and fatigue—without letting it define them. They move with change—anchored in purpose, yet fluid in approach.

The Strength of Vulnerable Influence

Vulnerability is often mischaracterized as weakness—especially in crisis. But in truth, it is a profound expression of strength. Relationally courageous leaders name pain without relinquishing hope. They are open about their humanity—and in doing so, they cultivate trust.

As Brené Brown reminds us, vulnerability is not the absence of strength—it is the expression of it. It says, "I feel this too, and I'm still here with you." It declares, "We may not have every answer, but we will move forward—together."

This is not performance. It is grounded authenticity. And through it, leaders create the conditions for authentic connection and collective courage.

The Team That Reclaimed Psychological Safety

At a global tech firm, a product team was quietly unraveling. Feedback sessions turned silent. Turnover crept up. The new team lead scrapped performance reviews for one quarter and replaced them with "feedback feasts"—intentional, emotionally attuned spaces where every voice was heard. No metrics. Just human check-ins. Trust returned. The next product sprint was the fastest in two years.

His Mosaic Intelligence in action:

Emotional Integrity: He led with authenticity, not output.
Cultural Flexibility: He adjusted tone and timing to meet global team norms.
Identity Agility: He moved from a performance lens to a presence lens.

Restoring Trust After a Crisis

Mistakes are inevitable in pressure-filled moments. But attuned leaders do not shy away from repair. They take responsibility, identify what went wrong, and invite reconnection.

Repair does not require perfection—it requires emotional availability. It sounds like:

"I see how this impacted you. I want to improve."

"This moment taught me something, and I am committed to rebuilding trust."

Trust isn't restored through explanation. It is rebuilt through accountability, consistency, and care.

Sustaining the Leader: The Emotional Toll of Holding Space

Leaders who make emotional space for others often struggle to find it for themselves. Over time, this leads to quiet, chronic depletion. Without clear emotional boundaries, even the strongest leaders face burnout.

Sustainability begins with inner work. Emotionally grounded leaders decompress after hard decisions, articulate their emotions with trusted confidants, and grant themselves permission to rest.

They also reject the myth of emotional flawlessness. You can be strong and still need support. Wise and still feel weary. You are not a machine—you are a mirror. And to reflect peace, you must tend to your own storms.

Leadership That Soothes the Storm

Every generation faces defining moments—seasons of disruption that test our beliefs and reshape our vision of what it means to lead others well.

In our time, emotional attunement is no longer a leadership accessory—it is an essential competency.

It is what distinguishes those who simply manage crisis from those who calm it.

Those who react from fear, from those who respond with presence.

Those who preserve control, from those who protect connection.

This is the moment for a different kind of leadership—one that soothes the storm not by silencing it, but by standing steady in the center of it.

The leaders who endure are not only strategic—they are present. They move through chaos with grace, speak with compassion, and offer steadiness when others falter. Crisis doesn't disqualify you. It refines you.

If you let it, it will shape you into the kind of leader the world needs now—steady, grounded, and profoundly human.

Insights from a Strong Support Network

In every crisis I have faced—whether personal, professional, or emotional—there has been one consistent stabilizing force that has made the difference between unraveling and rising: a strong support system.

Emotional fluency involves more than just self-regulation. It also encompasses knowing when to lean on others, recognizing who to call, and understanding whose steady energy calms you when your thoughts are spiraling, your breath is shallow, and your vision feels clouded.

I have witnessed support transform moments of chaos into clarity. Sometimes, it is not the absence of the storm that matters—it is the grounding attunement of people who remind you that you are not alone in it. People who do not need you to perform, who respect your strength but also welcome your softness, who will not let you spiral into isolation but will never shame you for struggling.

There are a few key people in my life—mentors, colleagues, trusted friends—who are more than sounding boards. They are anchors. They don't just celebrate my victories; they help shoulder the invisible weight when guidance becomes heavy. They remind me of who I am when I begin to forget. They bring emotional clarity into spaces where confusion tries to take root.

And this is not unique to me.

Across industries and identities, I've witnessed this quiet pattern. High-performing professionals, elite athletes, visionary creatives, and bold entrepreneurs all seem to share the same often-overlooked advantage: a strong emotional circle.

Not just networks or contacts—but soul-level allies.

People who speak truth with tenderness.

Who challenge without shaming.

Who show up not for performance, but for presence.

The emotionally attuned leader in a crisis doesn't pretend to carry it all alone. They reach out—not for optics, but for sustainability. They understand something many still overlook: that influence, especially in times of profound change, is not a solo act.

It is a collective practice.

Sometimes, it is even a sacred one.

If we hope to lead through crisis with integrity, we must build our support systems with the same intentionality we bring to our strategies. We need those who can hold space without rushing to fix. Who can remain present in tension. Who know that real leadership is not about certainty—it is about steadiness, surrender, and shared humanity.

Because in uncertain times, your strength won't just come from your skill set.

It will come from your circle.

The emotionally grounded architect does not deny their need for support—they embrace it. And in doing so, they model a new kind of presence:

One rooted in humility, shaped by resilience, and sustained by the quiet power of being held.

THE EMOTIONALLY ATTUNED LEADER IN CRISIS

Crisis doesn't create your leadership style—it reveals it. These prompts are designed to ground you when pressure rises, helping you reflect on how you lead under stress and who you depend on when strength alone isn't enough. In times of uncertainty, emotional steadiness becomes your most powerful tool.

- When has a moment of crisis revealed something essential about your leadership style or emotional habits?
- What does your team feel from you during high-stress situations—panic, grounded calm, silence, or steadiness?
- Who is part of your emotional support circle—and how intentionally are you cultivating those relationships?
- In a moment of crisis, how can you balance assertive leadership with cultural sensitivity and emotional safety for diverse stakeholders?

When the storm comes, your calm becomes the shelter.

Reconnecting with Others

We were never meant to face this alone.
Relationships are where we break—and where we rebuild.
Where we lose our way—and rediscover it again.

Let this be the moment
you lead with empathy,
listen without armor,
and speak with truth and tenderness.

Connection is the courage
to be seen
and to fully see others.

PART III

EMOTIONAL RESONANCE AS A TOOL FOR HEALING AND JUSTICE

Healing is emotional work. Justice is emotional labor. This section explores how emotional literacy deepens our capacity to confront harm, embrace truth, and lead in ways that restore—not just respond. It invites us to shift from performance to authenticity in the pursuit of equity and repair.

CHAPTER 11

Emotional Resonance for Social Justice

Emotional insight is often viewed as a personal growth tool—an inward journey that deepens self-understanding, strengthens relationships, and builds emotional resilience. However, it also serves a more urgent, collective purpose: the pursuit of justice.

In a world shaped by inequity—where systems privilege some and oppress others, where history remains unhealed, and where truth is often silenced—emotional fluency emerges as a transformative force. Change does not arise from policy and protest alone; it is also born in the quiet courage to engage emotionally, reflect deeply, and connect authentically amid reckoning.

Why is emotional literacy essential in the context of justice? Justice is not only structural; it is also emotional. It requires us to confront what we might prefer to ignore, recognize what we were never taught to see, and remain present in conversations that make us profoundly uncomfortable. It demands listening without defensiveness, acknowledging harm without retreating into shame, and creating space for accountability without dehumanization. These are not merely political skills; they are emotional ones.

Emotional fluency must evolve from a personal practice into a collective ethic to foster progress—not just to implement equity, but to embody it. It should influence how we lead, teach, hire, include, and heal.

Justice Requires Emotional Maturity

Justice requires emotional literacy—the ability to name, hold, and express difficult emotions with clarity. It also demands emotional maturity, the willingness to stay present amid discomfort rather than retreat into defensiveness.

One of the most significant barriers to justice is emotional fragility. Conversations about race, gender, power, or identity often trigger defensiveness, guilt, or withdrawal. These reactions—though sometimes unconscious—can hinder progress and reinforce the very systems we aim to change. It is not enough to believe in fairness; we must cultivate the emotional maturity to confront unfairness.

The Pillars of Emotional Capacity

This maturity is built on the pillars of emotional capacity. Inner awareness reveals biases, blind spots, and inherited patterns. Emotional regulation helps us endure discomfort rather than escape it. Relational intelligence enables us to connect with and support others whose lived experiences differ from our own. Purpose-driven motivation sustains our commitment to change. Social fluency translates our inner clarity into external impact—through dialogue, collaboration, and advocacy.

These are not theoretical virtues; they are essential capacities for justice-centered leadership.

Attunement Beyond Sympathy: Understanding the Whole Person

In justice work, emotional attunement is not pity—that is sympathy. True attunement recognizes the whole person and dares to confront the systems that render them invisible. It says, "I am willing to understand your world—and I care enough to change mine in response."

This shift—from observation to courageous engagement—transforms everything. It moves us from performative inclusion to genuine transformation. And nowhere is this more vital than in leadership.

Without empathy, leaders may unintentionally perpetuate harm—through exclusionary policies, silencing cultures, or feedback that ignores lived context. But when leaders lead with emotional resonance, they create environments where people feel not only seen and heard, but deeply understood. Resonance deepens trust, makes authenticity safe, and turns justice into a lived experience—not just a goal.

Leadership rooted in emotional depth doesn't simply include—it restores, reimagines, and transforms.

The Emotional Weight of Injustice

For those in marginalized communities, emotional insight is not merely a leadership tool—it serves as a lifeline. Being overlooked, underestimated, or tokenized entails invisible labor: code-switching, overperformance, and the emotional burden of constantly justifying one's own humanity. While emotional fluency can support individuals in managing these challenges, it must never be used to normalize or excuse them.

Too often, those who are harmed are expected to educate, soothe, and maintain composure. Emotional regulation cannot be the sole responsibility of those who suffer. It is a shared task. Individuals with privilege must develop the capacity to sit in discomfort, acknowledge harm, and center marginalized voices—without ego, defensiveness, or the need for recognition.

Emotional Regulation When Confronted with Truth

One of the most challenging emotional skills in justice work is regulating our emotions when faced with our own complicity. Whether you are an educator who focused on one narrative, an executive observing a lack of diversity, or a parent who overlooked a child's identity, those moments sting—and they should. However, shame is not a strategy, and silence is not a solution.

The emotionally attuned response is grounded humility: saying, "I missed that, and I am listening now"; admitting, "I did not realize the impact, and I want to do better"; and affirming, "I am open to learning from voices other than my own." This kind of self-regulation leads not to flawlessness, but to meaningful progress.

Emotional Presence at Work: Transforming Systems

What does emotionally fluent justice look like?

In schools, it manifests through trauma-informed teaching, culturally responsive curricula, and the inclusion of student voices in decision-making. In workplaces, it's visible in equitable hiring practices, inclusive leadership development, and listening sessions that spark real policy reform.

In healthcare, it respects the lived experiences behind the diagnoses. In government, it prioritizes people—not just metrics. In families, it makes room for difficult conversations about difference—without shame or silence.

It begins with emotional honesty—the courage to ask:
How do people feel in this space?
Whose voice is absent?
What are we willing to change in response?

Creating Space for Collective Healing

Justice is not only about recognizing harm—it is also about creating space for healing. And healing cannot occur in emotionally unsafe environments.

Emotionally present communities hold space for grief, anger, and truth—not sanitized, but acknowledged. They allow multiple truths to coexist. They understand that healing is not linear, and that dignity must precede reconciliation.

This is especially important across generations and cultures. Elders may bear wounds that remain unnamed. Young individuals may carry an urgency that goes unspoken. Emotional literacy builds the bridge—inviting dialogue without correction, healing without erasure.

The Role of Leaders in Promoting Justice

Leaders must be architects of trust and transparency—not perfect, but present. Justice-centered leadership requires acknowledging harm when it is easier to overlook it; listening when silence feels safer; and taking public responsibility when private discomfort tempts one to deflect.

It involves creating space—for grief, for repair, and for co-creation—not simply updating policies or issuing statements. Most importantly, it signifies being a learner in public. Leaders who demonstrate vulnerability and growth invite others to do the same.

Personal Reflections: Justice as an Emotional Journey

For many of us, the call to justice did not begin with policy. It began with a moment, a story, and a voice we could not unhear. For me, it started with conversations that challenged my assumptions and environments that disrupted my comfort. Justice demanded my unlearning and my rehumanizing.

It urged me not to be right, but to be ready. Ready to listen. Ready to change. Ready to step aside or step forward. The journey has been uncomfortable yet sacred. Justice involves not only transforming systems but also transforming the people within them.

The Inner Work That Makes Outer Change Possible

If we desire justice to endure, we must be willing to go deep. We must move beyond performance, beyond posture, and into authenticity. We must be willing to feel what has gone numb, to lift what has been dropped, and to restore what has been broken.

Emotional integrity is not a cure-all. However, it is the foundation that gives justice its heart. It ensures that our movements are not only loud but also loving; not only urgent but also anchored.

The question isn't, "Am I emotionally fluent enough to contribute to justice?"

The real question is, "Am I willing to let justice transform how I feel, how I lead, how I live—and to lead from *that* place?"

Because that is where real change begins.

Lessons from Being the "Only One": The Burden and Insight of Leadership

One of the most unspoken realities of influence is what it means to be the only one in the room—the only woman, the only Black woman, the only voice representing a specific truth, identity, or lived experience. I have held that role—with quiet power—in spaces where my very presence challenged the status quo.

Being the only one is not about ego. It speaks to the emotional and cultural labor of carrying those who are absent. You become a translator, a bridge, and a conscience—shouldering the hopes of your community while navigating the complexities of representation, often without a roadmap.

Many of my peers—especially Black women in positions of influence—know this weight intimately. Our visibility signals progress, but it also underscores how far we still have to go. Representation matters—but without empathy, equity, and systemic awareness, it becomes a symbol with no soul.

The barriers we face are often not personal; they are generational and structural. Emotional insight equips us to recognize these systems, name their impact, and continue to lead within them—without losing ourselves in the process.

Over time, I've learned to listen differently—to pay attention not just to who is speaking, but to who is being dismissed. This is emotional fluency at its highest expression: hearing what isn't said, holding space for voices long silenced by tradition or hierarchy, and creating openings for presence, not just participation.

This is the essence of justice-centered leadership —not inclusion in rhetoric, but inclusion in practice. It's about cultivating environments where people feel safe enough to speak, empowered enough to grow, and valued enough to stay.

Because when people feel invisible, they leave. They disengage. They seek safety elsewhere. They protect their peace by stepping away.

Justice-centered presence doesn't require us to fix everything.

It calls us to tell the truth about what is broken—and to stop pretending all is well.

It asks us to be bold enough to ask who's missing—and honest enough to notice who's carrying too much.

Being the only one taught me to lead with both strength and softness. It reminded me that while I may be the first and the only, I will never be the last. Every courageous act of speaking makes space for others to be seen.

Reflection

EMOTIONAL RESONANCE FOR SOCIAL JUSTICE

Lasting change begins within. These prompts invite you to examine how your emotions shape your ability to engage in justice—not just through action, but through authenticity, empathy, and sustained commitment. Justice without emotional maturity can devolve into performance. However, justice rooted in emotional integrity leads to transformation.

- Where have your emotions blocked your ability to engage in justice—and where could they deepen your empathy?
- Whose absence have you become emotionally numb to—and how can you begin to notice again?
- What discomfort are you willing to sit with so that healing, inclusion, and change become possible?
- How can your emotional fluency support equity and inclusion within your leadership spaces?

Emotional integrity doesn't make justice easier—it makes it more human.

CHAPTER 12

Healing Generational and Cultural Wounds

We do not arrive in this world as blank slates. We are born into stories that are already unfolding—shaped by culture, community, and the generations that preceded us. Some of these stories empower us, while others wound us; most contain elements of both. Although we may not be responsible for everything we inherit, we are accountable for what we choose to carry forward.

Healing generational and cultural wounds requires more than knowledge. It demands emotional insight—the clarity to recognize what we have unconsciously absorbed, the regulation to endure discomfort without retreating, and the empathy to rebuild relationships across time, space, and identity. This work is not only deeply personal; it is profoundly transformational. It is the labor of love that enables us to envision and create a more harmonious future.

These wounds often reside quietly within us. They manifest in the ways we love, cope, lead, and parent. They appear in our silences, in unexamined traditions, and in beliefs transmitted not through words, but through survival. Emotional fluency allows us to notice these patterns—not with judgment, but with awareness. And awareness is where healing begins.

The Emotional Legacy Passed Down Through Generations

Every family, culture, and community carries emotional patterns—both spoken and unspoken. In some homes, emotions are explored and expressed, while in others, they remain hidden behind silence or shame. Some cultures value emotional openness; others perceive vulnerability as a threat to survival. Some pass down resilience through storytelling, while others do so through sacrifice, duty, or quiet endurance.

All of these contribute to our emotional blueprint—how we feel, what we suppress, and how we relate to others. If we do not examine these emotional legacies, we risk repeating them. What our grandparents feared, we may still avoid. What they could not express, we may continue to silence. What they lost, we might unwittingly spend our lives trying to restore.

Emotional wholeness breaks that cycle. It provides us with a voice for the unspoken, tools for what once overwhelmed us, and the courage to become what our ancestors never had the opportunity to be—whole. This should not be mistaken for a betrayal of the past; rather, it is a blessing for the future.

Culture and the Complexity of Emotion

Culture profoundly shapes our expressions, interpretations, and responses to emotions. In one culture, eye contact signals respect; in another, it suggests disrespect. In some families, vulnerability is seen as strength, while in others, it is considered weakness. These cultural codes are powerful and often invisible—until we enter spaces that challenge them.

I encountered this truth in real time while living and working in the Middle East. Coming from a Western background that celebrated individual expression, I had to learn to navigate an Eastern framework rooted in modesty, collective identity, and deep respect. What I initially perceived as emotional restraint revealed itself as quiet strength. What seemed distant transformed into dignified thoughtfulness.

That experience reshaped me. I became more emotionally fluent and culturally attuned. I realized that emotional adaptability is not a one-size-fits-all trait; rather, it is a dynamic and evolving skill—one that deepens as we navigate through diverse cultures, generations, and contexts.

For those of us with layered identities—those who speak multiple languages, hold several passports, or live between generations—this emotional navigation becomes even more nuanced. Emotional insight serves as our compass, grounding us in our values while remaining open to the values of others. It empowers us to honor our heritage without being confined by it and allows us to reconcile with the past while intentionally shaping the future.

Intergenerational Healing and Emotional Reparenting

Healing generational wounds often means learning to be the emotional adult your younger self needed—and your elders never had the chance to become. This work is sacred; it asks us to grieve what was missing while honoring what was endured.

Emotionally attuned healing does not aim to blame; it seeks to understand. It acknowledges the trauma, limitations, and survival instincts of previous generations—and then it chooses a new path. It offers gentleness where there was harshness, truth where there was silence, and emotional availability where there was absence.

This is emotional reparenting—not just for ourselves, but for our children, our students, and our teams. It is the quiet yet powerful decision to say, "The pain stops with me. Not because I am perfect, but because I am awake."

You might be the first to question why things have always been done in a certain way. The first to establish a boundary. The first to seek therapy. Although that work may feel isolating at times, it also marks the beginning of liberation—not just for you, but for every life that follows yours.

Leadership and the Responsibility of Emotional Legacy

Leadership goes beyond systems and strategy. It involves the emotional climate you cultivate, the behaviors you exemplify, and the culture you promote. Many organizations continue to function based on outdated generational norms—demanding loyalty without transparency, equating distance with professionalism, and prioritizing performance over well-being. These practices are not only ineffective; they are also harmful.

Emotionally attuned leaders challenge these assumptions. They understand that leadership is about more than outcomes—it's about emotional legacy. How will your team remember you? With fear or fairness? With control or compassion? For performance—or for the emotional impact you made?

Leaders who have undergone emotional healing lead differently. They do not replicate the systems that once harmed them, nor do they project their wounds onto others. They lead from a place of wholeness, creating cultures where safety, growth, and trust are not rare luxuries, but daily norms.

The Role of Storytelling in Cultural Healing

Stories are more than mere words; they are vessels for memory, emotion, and identity. Every culture shares stories to transmit wisdom, values, and survival strategies. When we listen to others' stories—or tell our own—we create space for healing. Listening becomes a sacred act—neither passive nor performative, but active and honoring. To listen with empathy is to convey, "You belong. Your story matters."

Stories create connections across generations and cultures. They reveal truths that cannot be quantified by data or illustrated in charts. In leadership, storytelling serves as a tool for trust, a way to foster connection, and an invitation for others to engage wholeheartedly.

Share your story. Reveal your family's truth—not only the highlights but also the healing. Encourage others to do the same. Then listen. Ask: What needs honoring? What needs releasing? What can be rewritten?

Building Bridges Across Generations

It is easy to critique older generations, but building bridges with them is harder—and more transformational. Every generation possesses wisdom and experiences its own wounds. Healing begins when we cease performing for one another and start listening—with curiosity—even when we disagree.

Younger generations should be free to challenge flawed systems, while older generations should be free to share how they endured them. Emotional fluency enables that exchange, inviting dialogue rather than debate, and valuing connection over control.

This work demands time, patience, and grace, but it is important. A society that forgets its elders loses its memory, while a society that silences its youth loses its imagination. We need both.

You Are the Turning Point

Whether you realize it or not, you are the turning point in your lineage. You are the bridge between what was and what will be. You possess the power to pass down something different—not idealism, but emotional grounding. Not pressure, but peace.

Emotional depth provides the tools to gently break generational cycles, speak the truth without shame, and heal while honoring your history. You may not have chosen the wounds you carry, but you can choose the legacy you leave behind.

Let that legacy reflect courage. Let it embody connection. Let it represent conscious healing. The future is shaped not only by what we build but also by what we heal.

Lessons in Slowing Down

I was taught early in my career that sacrifice was the ultimate sign of commitment. Sacrifice your time. Sacrifice your health. Sacrifice your family. Influence, I was told, meant being everywhere—always available, always on.

And for a long time, I believed it.

I wore exhaustion like a badge of honor. I equated long hours with impact, and urgency with value. I cared deeply for my team—but I ignored my own limits. The unspoken message was clear: compassion could exist, but not for yourself.

Everything shifted when my mother became ill.

Suddenly, the quiet voice within—the one that had long urged me to slow down—grew louder. The weight of my responsibilities, the reality of my family's needs, and the truth of my own emotional limits began to collide. I continued to lead—but I started asking different questions:

What is the cost of impact if it costs you yourself?

Who benefits from influence that punishes humanity?

Why do we glorify self-erasure and call it excellence?

Caring for my mother taught me what no seminar or strategy ever could: slowing down is not weakness—it is wisdom.

During that season, I chose to lead differently. I delegated more. I communicated transparently. I paused when I needed to. And to my surprise, the world did not fall apart. My presence, in fact, deepened.

My team responded not with criticism, but with compassion. They didn't disengage—they leaned in.

That's when I discovered something essential: vulnerability is not the opposite of guidance—it is what makes sustainable influence possible.

This wasn't just a personal turning point. It was a generational shift. I was interrupting a legacy of self-sacrifice and choosing to model a new one—one built on honesty, wholeness, and emotional alignment.

Healing does not always manifest through grand gestures. Sometimes, it emerges from quiet choices: choosing to rest, being honest, and allowing oneself to be seen—not just as a leader, but as a human being.

I still believe in excellence, but I no longer define it by burnout. The mission may be urgent, but the individuals behind it must be well. Emotional fluency has reminded me that I am not just a leader; I am a person. Honoring that truth has transformed everything. When leaders choose healing, they give others permission to do the same. That is how cultures change—not through pressure, but through emotional authenticity.

Reflection

HEALING GENERATIONAL AND CULTURAL WOUNDS

Some wounds are not merely personal—they are inherited. These prompts encourage you to explore what exists in your emotional lineage and to choose which aspects of that inheritance you are ready to release or reimagine. Healing is not just about the past—it is about how we shape the future with emotional courage.

- What emotional patterns were passed down to you, and which ones are you ready to release?
- How has your culture shaped your relationship with emotions—and where might that need reimagining?
- What legacy do you want to leave—not just through your work, but through your healing?
- Which unhealed generational or cultural wounds have shaped the way you include or exclude others—and how are you beginning to transform that?

Healing what came before you is one of the boldest ways to lead what comes next.

CHAPTER 13

Raising the Next Generation with Emotional Integrity

If relational and emotional fluency is the key to reshaping how we lead, heal, and connect, then raising the next generation with these values is not only essential—it's urgent. Building on the previous chapter's exploration of intergenerational and cultural healing, this chapter focuses on children: how we nurture their emotional development, and how we break cycles by learning to be the emotionally present adults they need.

We are not merely raising children; we are nurturing future partners, neighbors, parents, thinkers, and bridge builders. Emotional literacy is not just a skill we impart; it is a legacy we create. For many of us, it is a legacy we are learning to offer for the very first time.

The Emotional Blueprint Forms Early

Children begin developing an internal blueprint for understanding emotions from infancy. They absorb the emotional tone of their household and observe how adults handle frustration or joy. They learn whether their feelings are welcomed or dismissed. Neuroscience confirms that a child's early emotional experiences shape the architecture of the developing brain. The consistency or absence of attuned caregiving literally wires the brain for regulation or reactivity.

According to research from Harvard's Center on the Developing Child, consistent emotional attunement and co-regulation with caregivers enhance the brain's capacity for executive functioning, impulse control, and empathy. Children learn to feel by observing our emotions. They learn to regulate by experiencing regulation alongside us. They become emotionally aware when they witness it in practice.

This is not about perfect parenting; it is about present parenting. Being emotionally available—even if imperfectly—sends the message that emotion is safe, identifiable, and manageable.

Inclusive Parenting Begins at Home

Emotionally literate children do not emerge by accident—they are shaped by the modeling, language, and values they absorb at home. As caregivers, our job is not only to teach regulation, but to model inclusion. In a world where difference can provoke fear, it is our responsibility to raise children who are not only emotionally fluent but also inclusive, curious, and attuned to those who are different from them.

Inclusion starts early. When we name emotions, affirm different cultural norms, and make space for hard conversations, we lay the foundation for children who value belonging as much as bravery. Inclusive parenting is not about protecting children from discomfort—it is about equipping them to navigate it with empathy and courage.

When we practice emotional fluency at home, we are not just shaping emotionally healthy individuals—we are shaping future leaders capable of honoring complexity and holding space for others. Inclusion begins in the questions we ask, the stories we tell, and the moments we pause to listen.

Modeling Over Management

Many adults were raised in environments where emotional expression was discouraged, minimized, or misunderstood. We were taught to be strong, to stop crying, or to calm down—without ever being shown how. Consequently, we may carry an internal script that regards emotions as problems to solve or behaviors to correct.

Raising emotionally attuned children requires a shift from managing emotions to modeling them. Instead of silencing emotions or punishing outbursts, we begin to explore the unmet needs beneath them. We ground ourselves rather than react. We create space for the child's experience—not to excuse behavior, but to guide it.

This approach does not eliminate boundaries; it reinforces them. Emotionally responsive parenting isn't permissiveness; it involves being present with structure. It conveys that feelings are safe here while still emphasizing the importance of limits.

Children do not need unrealistic standards. They need adults who can remain calm when they cannot. They need adults who can articulate the experience of emotions in real time. They need someone to say, "I got frustrated too—and here's how I calmed my body." The most effective way to teach regulation is to model it aloud.

Repair Is More Powerful Than Perfection

Even the most emotionally aware adults can lose patience. We raise our voices, misinterpret situations, and bring our stress into the room. That is not failure; it is life.

What happens next, however, distinguishes a responsive household from a rigid one. Repair is the sacred act of reconnection after a rupture. Children remember repair more than they do mistakes.

When we kneel to their level, meet their eyes, and say, "I shouldn't have yelled. That wasn't your fault. I was overwhelmed, and I'm sorry," we build trust that no rule or reward system can replace.

Repair teaches accountability, humility, and emotional safety. It reminds children that love does not vanish when challenges arise—and that relationships can endure conflict.

We are beginning to see more schools model this shift—from correction to connection. One principal's approach became a turning point not only for discipline—but for dignity.

The Principal Who Replaced Detention with Dialogue

After a spike in behavioral referrals, a middle school principal launched "Restoration Fridays." Instead of detention, students joined facilitated reflection circles. They wrote letters of responsibility, explored emotional triggers, and practiced re-entry rituals with teachers. Suspensions dropped by forty percent in one semester—not because discipline disappeared, but because dignity returned.

Her Mosaic Intelligence in action:

Emotional Integrity: She named harm without shame.
Cultural Flexibility: She honored the diversity of how students express pain.
Identity Agility: She shifted from being an enforcer to a restorative leader.

Enhancing Emotional Vocabulary

You cannot process what you cannot name. Many children and adults lack the emotional vocabulary required to comprehend or express their inner world.

Emotionally conscious families prioritize this language. They teach children to distinguish between anger, disappointment, and feeling overwhelmed. Naming emotions becomes the first step toward understanding them. Over time, these words become tools for resilience and clarity.

This emotional fluency empowers children, providing them with a deeper understanding of themselves and others. It also fosters self-awareness, which serves as a foundation for healthy relationships and maturity.

Cultural and Generational Factors

Raising emotionally conscious children requires us to consider the cultural and generational contexts in which they are growing. In many cultures, emotional expression has been controlled or silenced as a means of survival. Certain emotions were seen as weak, dangerous, or disrespectful.

For many caregivers, raising emotionally open children is not only unfamiliar but also uncomfortable. It may feel like a rejection of tradition.

But emotional responsiveness does not reject culture; it enhances it. We can honor tradition while also allowing for vulnerability. We can ground emotional development in rituals such as storytelling, music, prayer, and movement. We can exemplify strength through reflection rather than suppression.

For those raising children in different cultures, emotional fluency serves as a thread of belonging. Through immigration, adoption, or global transitions, emotionally attuned caregiving fosters safety—even when identity feels complex.

Cross-cultural parenting and teaching require discernment. During my time in the Middle East, I experienced this firsthand. Silence surrounded certain topics—pain was managed privately, not publicly. Once, I attempted to create space for dialogue after a family tragedy and was gently informed that I had overstepped my bounds. The pain was not meant to be spoken aloud. I had misinterpreted the emotional language of the environment.

That experience taught me that emotional fluency across cultures is not just about expression; it is also about discernment—knowing when to speak, when to listen, and when silence is the highest form of respect.

The Role of Schools and Educators

Educators play a vital role in nurturing emotional development. Many students spend more of their waking hours with teachers than with their caregivers. A teacher's emotional attunement significantly influences a child's sense of safety and self-worth.

Schools prioritizing social and emotional learning do not just manage behavior—they transform lives. Students in emotionally attuned classrooms achieve better academically, foster healthier relationships, and regulate themselves more effectively.

But emotional growth in education is not merely a curriculum; it is an attitude. It manifests in how a teacher greets a student, addresses disruptions, and exhibits calm under pressure. Emotionally mature educators do more than teach; they become emotional anchors for children who may have never found safety elsewhere.

Preparing Children for a Disrupted World

We are raising children in a world of constant disruption—a world that requires emotional agility and inner clarity. The old models of silence, shame, and suppression no longer benefit them.

Our children must learn to hold grief and hope simultaneously, to advocate without losing themselves, and to articulate their pain while understanding that it does not define them.

Children who develop emotional maturity lead with empathy, pause before reacting, and set boundaries without guilt. They provide safety to others because they have found safety within themselves.

Becoming the People We Need

Most of us are raising children while still healing ourselves. We are breaking cycles we did not choose, parenting without a blueprint. That is emotional leadership in its truest form.

Each time you pause instead of yelling, repair instead of retreating, and acknowledge your own emotions instead of avoiding them, you are not merely teaching; you are transforming. You are growing into the person you needed and imparting that wholeness to the next generation.

You don't need to be perfect. You just need to stay present. That groundedness is what they will remember.

Lessons from the Classroom: Guiding, Not Controlling Emotional Development

One of the greatest insights I've gained about raising emotionally aware children didn't stem from theory—it emerged from the classroom. Over the years, I've had the privilege of teaching, mentoring, and guiding hundreds of students. Time and again, I've witnessed the same truth unfold: children and teens test boundaries—not because they are broken, but because they are still evolving.

Yes, some students arrive with significant emotional needs. They carry trauma, instability, or unmet attachments. Some seek validation, while others challenge boundaries. Occasionally, they may even use emotional safety to avoid accountability. Still, we must remember: they are learning. They are not finished. Our role as adults is not to excuse every behavior, but to honor the developmental journey unfolding before us.

I've had students who challenged me deeply. But I've also seen many of them grow into adults—building families and stepping into the role of mentors themselves. And I now understand: they were absorbing. They were shaping their own emotional world based on how we responded when they were struggling.

That's the heart of raising and educating emotionally aware children. They push. They test. But each moment offers an invitation: to model calm, extend grace, correct with care, and lead with grounded compassion.

In both classroom and home, structure and compassion must go hand in hand. Boundaries are expressions of care. Emotional expression is not the enemy—but unchecked chaos is. One of the greatest gifts we can offer children is space: space to feel, to explore, and to be guided gently back to truth and responsibility.

Children don't need perfect adults. They need reliable ones. Safe ones. Those who meet emotional tests with strength and grace.

If we want to raise emotionally attuned children, we must become emotionally mature adults. We should hold the mirror—not to shame, but to shape. Every misaligned moment is an opportunity to lead.

When we lead well, we create a legacy that outlasts us.

What we model in our homes becomes the first blueprint for Mosaic Intelligence. When we lead our children with emotional integrity, cultural sensitivity, and identity awareness, we are not only raising emotionally literate individuals—we are nurturing future leaders equipped to build a more connected, compassionate world.

Reflection

RAISING THE NEXT GENERATION WITH EMOTIONAL INTEGRITY

Every interaction with a child is an opportunity to model emotional integrity. These prompts invite you to reflect on the emotional messages you're sending—both spoken and unspoken—and how to create an environment where the next generation learns not only to feel, but to feel with wisdom, courage, and safety.

- What emotional lessons are you passing down—intentionally or unintentionally?
- When was the last time you repaired after an emotional rupture with a child or teen?
- How can you create a safer emotional climate for the next generation—without sacrificing structure or boundaries?
- How are you teaching emotional fluency that affirms difference, fosters inclusion, and strengthens your child's sense of identity and belonging?
- How are you modeling the kind of emotionally inclusive leadership you want children to inherit?

Emotionally attuned children are raised by emotionally present adults.

Toward Emotional Healing and Social Transformation

Healing is not gentle.
It is courageous.
It is unsettling.
It is sacred.

We cannot transform the world
without first acknowledging the truth about it.

This is where pain transforms into wisdom,
where grief evolves into movement,
and where justice takes root in the heart.
May this mark your bold beginning.

PART IV

DESIGNING THE FUTURE WITH EQ

The future is being built every day—in classrooms, on screens, and in spaces where culture is shaped. This section examines how emotional resonance must be integrated into systems, technology, and design to create environments where connection, creativity, and care can thrive.

CHAPTER 14

Emotional Presence in the Digital Age

We are the most connected generation in history—and, in many ways, the most emotionally distant. Technology has enabled us to reach across the world in seconds; yet, many of us struggle to connect with the person sitting next to us. We can send messages instantly, but our understanding often lags behind. We are exposed to more emotion than ever, yet we process it less meaningfully.

This paradox defines much of modern life. The digital age has transformed how we work, communicate, relate, and lead. It has granted us access to opportunity, creativity, and knowledge on a global scale. Yet, it has also introduced new challenges to our emotional well-being: digital fatigue, disembodied communication, online conflict, and the erosion of authenticity. In this landscape, emotional fluency and resilience are not merely helpful—they are essential.

We can no longer afford to separate emotional awareness from digital fluency. We must learn to lead, teach, and live with emotional clarity in digital spaces—not as a retreat from humanity but as an extension of it.

The Emotional Impact of Constant Connectivity

Technology was meant to simplify life, yet for many, it has complicated emotional management. The relentless pace of digital existence—emails, texts, notifications, meetings, and news cycles—maintains our nervous systems in a state of low-grade hyperarousal. We are perpetually "on," always reachable, and seldom fully present.

Research by the American Psychological Association indicates that constant connectivity can elevate stress and hinder our ability to self-regulate. The dopamine feedback loops ingrained in social media favor reaction over reflection, promoting speed over depth. Studies from the University of Pennsylvania and the Massachusetts Institute of Technology confirm that high levels of social media use are linked to increased anxiety, loneliness, and emotional comparison.

In this context, emotional regulation is not just a personal skill—it's a survival strategy. Emotionally aware individuals learn to pause before responding, set intentional screen-time boundaries, and bring mindfulness into their digital interactions.

Without intention, technology doesn't just consume our time—it erodes our emotional focus.

Digital Communication and the Loss of Nuance

One significant loss of digital communication is nuance. Facial expressions, pauses, posture, and tone of voice—all essential for emotional understanding—are frequently missing in virtual conversations. Consequently, meanings can become distorted. A brief message might feel cold. A delayed response may provoke insecurity. A misunderstood comment can spark unnecessary conflict.

Digitally attuned communicators understand this risk. They clarify tone and follow up when messages feel unclear. They ask questions like, "How did that land for you?" to ensure that digital interactions do not sacrifice emotional connection.

In virtual meetings, emotionally attuned leaders make space for more than updates—they create moments of emotional resonance.

They ask, "How are you—really?" and stay present long enough to hear the truth. In a digital world that often flattens connection, resonance brings depth back into the conversation. It reminds us that human presence isn't about proximity—it's about emotional availability.

The Rise of Digital Conflict and the Erosion of Compassion

Social media has created an unprecedented space for expression, but it has also eroded compassionate awareness. Behind screens, people forget that there are humans on the other side. Conflict escalates quickly; empathy collapses. Outrage becomes performative.

Digital anonymity dissolves the social accountability we experience in person. People type what they'd never say face-to-face. Even well-intentioned conversations can spiral without the context that body language and tone provide.

Digitally responsible communication offers an alternative. It doesn't shy away from difficult conversations—it engages with emotional clarity, curiosity, and care. It means pausing before reacting, choosing reflection over reactivity, and remembering that every post, message, and comment carries an emotional backdrop.

We must understand the difference between inviting someone to a conversation and calling someone out for their performance. Digital spaces should be arenas for humanity, not merely for hostility.

The Importance of Emotional Boundaries in a Digital World

The digital world has blurred boundaries—between work and rest, home and office, personal and professional. Our phones follow us into every room. Notifications disrupt our moments of peace, and the emotional toll is real.

Without boundaries, burnout becomes unavoidable. Emotional availability turns into emotional depletion. Moreover, the effort of perpetual responsiveness exhausts even the most resilient leaders and caregivers.

Emotionally attuned boundaries are liberating. They are not barriers—they are containers for clarity. They protect your emotional energy and empower you to show up more fully when it matters most.

These boundaries might look like tech-free dinners, scheduled log-off times, or intentional limits on digital notifications. They might also sound like, "I am offline after 7 p.m.," or "I need space before responding to this message."

Boundaries represent acts of self-leadership. They protect our grounded awareness. In a fast-paced world, they teach us to honor our limits with grace.

The Significance of Emotional Attunement in Virtual Leadership

Leadership in the digital age requires greater emotional attunement than ever before. It is no longer enough to assign tasks or share goals. Leaders must build trust, foster belonging, and express care—through a screen.

This means celebrating wins, checking in with team members, and recognizing invisible labor. It involves noticing who has grown quiet, following up when someone disengages, and making space for connection—not just output.

And perhaps most importantly, it means modeling humanity: "Here's what I'm feeling today—and here's how I'm navigating it."

Remote work does not have to equate to remote emotion. Attuned leaders radiate warmth, emotional steadiness, and presence—even in virtual environments.

Digital Culture and Generational Intelligence

Different generations engage with digital life in distinct ways. Baby Boomers often favor structured communication and face-to-face interaction. Millennials blend emotional openness with digital fluency. Generation Z expresses depth through memes, voice notes, and short-form visuals—distilling emotion into compact, creative formats.

Emotionally fluent leadership embraces these differences. It honors generational expression and makes space for emotional diversity across platforms. Cultural and generational humility becomes essential. What one generation calls oversharing, another sees as vulnerability. What one calls disengagement, another identifies as overstimulation.

An emotionally attuned response is not rooted in judgment—it is shaped by curiosity. It seeks to translate across generational lines and build bridges that foster understanding rather than alienation.

Human-Centered Design: Aligning Technology with Emotional Needs

Technology must evolve to support emotional well-being. Platforms can be designed with emotional fluency in mind. Small choices—like pause-before-post features, delayed sending, emotional check-ins, or calming visual aesthetics—can create transformative impact.

Some companies are already paving the way, building emotionally responsive digital ecosystems that minimize harm and promote care. But this should not be the exception. It must become the norm.

We cannot outsource empathy to artificial intelligence. But we can—and must—embed emotional awareness into every layer of the digital experience: from interface to algorithm, from leadership to culture.

Rethinking Presence in a Digitally Saturated World

Connection is not about physical proximity—it is about intentional presence. You can sit beside someone and still feel emotionally distant. And you can be thousands of miles apart yet deeply connected—if your heart and attention are attuned.

Relational awareness asks:
"Am I truly here?"
"Am I engaging with care?"
"Am I reacting—or relating?"

Focused attention is a gift we offer others—but it's also a gift we give ourselves. In a world of constant distraction, intentional emotional engagement is a radical act of clarity and care.

Remaining Human in a Digital World

The digital world is not the enemy; it is a new frontier—one that holds both promise and peril. The challenge is not to abandon technology but to remain fully human within it. Relational awareness serves as the compass that helps us navigate this world without losing ourselves.

It reminds us to slow down, to check in, and to invite back in the person behind the profile. It calls us to lead with grounded empathy and to choose care in moments when judgment feels easier.

Let us not build a future that connects us more while understanding us less. Let us bring our entire selves into digital spaces—not perfectly, but purposefully. Because in the end, emotional insight will not only make our digital lives more manageable, but also more meaningful.

The Digital Shift: Redefining Communication and Leadership for Diverse Personality Types

One of the most inspiring evolutions I've witnessed in this era of digital transformation is the redefinition of influence—particularly through the lens of communication.

With the rise of remote work, messaging platforms, and asynchronous collaboration, we've seen a long-overdue expansion of space for introverted guides to step forward in ways that feel both authentic and sustainable. This shift has not been a trend—it's been a restoration. A necessary evolution.

I've had the privilege of working alongside brilliant, thoughtful, and steady contributors whose voices were once overlooked in more extroverted environments. Their emergence represents more than just a change in tone—it embodies a new model of presence, and a deep well of wisdom from which we can all draw.

But if I'm honest, this transition hasn't always been seamless for me.

As a natural extrovert, I process life through conversation. I thrive on energy, real-time interaction, and spontaneous exchange. I lead by relating—by engaging in the moment and listening with my full self. Navigating the digital and hybrid landscape has required me to bridge the space between immediacy and introspection. I've had to recalibrate—learning to hold space for quieter, more reflective ways of leading that are equally powerful.

Even as styles diversify, one truth remains: human connection is still the glue.

Digital tools offer access—but they also blur emotional clarity. A team channel message may not carry tone. A muted Zoom square can conceal pain. In these moments, it's the emotional resonance—the timing, the trust, the attuned communication—that binds us.

Sustainable influence in the digital age is not about volume.

It's about emotional precision.

The challenge is this: how can we honor different communication styles while maintaining the warmth and trust that only genuine connection can foster?

Emotional presence is essential for navigating this shift. It isn't about forcing introverts into extroverted roles or asking extroverts to tone down their gifts. It's about creating emotionally aware spaces where all communication styles are acknowledged, valued, and respected. Voice still matters. Emotional engagement still matters. And regardless of personality type, your team needs to feel that you are with them—not just behind a screen, but actively attuned and available.

Behind-Screen Leadership and Digital Bullying

In this digital era, a subtle yet dangerous behavior has emerged—screen-shielded leadership. This tendency, observed among some individuals, including those in power, involves using the distance of the screen as a shield. It serves as a way to evade accountability, assert dominance, or micromanage without the responsibility of genuine dialogue. This behavior does not always manifest through dramatic outbursts. More often, it appears as emotional unavailability, passive-aggressive messages, silence when clarity is needed, or pressure exerted through platforms instead of conversation.

This is also a crisis of emotional fluency.

We must not allow digital tools to foster unchecked behavior or radical personality shifts that undermine psychological safety. A respectful tone and emotional steadiness must remain non-negotiable—whether in person or online. The screen should never serve as an escape route for cruelty or manipulation.

Emotionally accountable cultures require digital responsibility, not just digital access.

Leaders should exemplify this from the top.

The Future of Leadership Is Digital— but It Must Remain Human.

Communication is not about volume; it is about resonance. Great leadership is not about visibility—it is about emotional availability.

Whether introverted or extroverted, remote or in person—your emotional availability still matters. Your empathy matters. Your voice, when rooted in care, remains the most powerful digital tool you possess. No matter how advanced the technology becomes, emotional depth will always be the bridge.

Reflection

EMOTIONAL PRESENCE IN THE DIGITAL AGE

The speed of technology often outpaces the depth of our emotions. These prompts invite you to reflect on how your emotional attentiveness manifests—or fades—within digital spaces. Whether you're leading a virtual team, sending a late-night message, or scrolling through endless updates, your ability to lead with warmth and intention remains essential.

- When was the last time you felt emotionally disconnected in a digital interaction—and what might have restored presence?
- What habits—urgency, overexplanation, silence, or tone—do you carry into online spaces that may need reflection or refinement?
- Where in your digital leadership or relationships could you reintroduce warmth, intentionality, or human connection?
- How are you using digital spaces to model inclusive presence and emotionally intelligent discourse?

In a digital world, emotional presence is not diminished—it is needed more than ever.

CHAPTER 15

Designing Emotionally Responsive Spaces

Emotional awareness, initially a personal practice, achieves its greatest impact when it transcends the individual and permeates the environments we inhabit. This transformation is not only inspiring—it is revolutionary. Individuals with emotional fluency can foster moments of connection, while emotionally attuned spaces possess the ability to cultivate cultures of trust, instilling a sense of reassurance and confidence.

This chapter is about transformation—from individual skill to systemic design. It explores how we embed emotional capacity into our institutions, classrooms, workplaces, communities, and homes. It focuses on designing environments where empathy is not exceptional but expected and valued. Where regulation is not reactive but modeled. Where belonging is not a buzzword—it is built into the foundation, sparking engagement and interest, making everyone feel included and valued.

Emotional development should no longer be relegated to personal growth seminars or optional training. It must be integrated into how we structure our experiences—because structure influences behavior, and behavior shapes culture.

The Influence of Emotionally Attuned Environments

We have long understood that emotionally attuned individuals tend to experience deeper relationships, greater resilience, and higher life satisfaction. But what happens when emotional fluency is embedded not just in individuals—but in the very architecture of a space, team, or system?

Research from the Center for Creative Leadership shows that organizations with high emotional awareness at every level—from executive presence to frontline guidance—experience significantly stronger employee engagement, reduced turnover, and elevated team performance.

A 2020 study published in *Frontiers in Psychology* further revealed that emotionally fluent guidance is directly linked to higher levels of psychological safety, creativity, and innovation across industries.

In education, classrooms infused with social-emotional learning cultivate student well-being. According to the Collaborative for Academic, Social, and Emotional Learning (CASEL), schools that integrate SEL programs show an average eleven percent increase in academic outcomes. Emotional safety enhances learning, especially for students navigating trauma, cultural disconnection, or systemic inequity.

In healthcare, emotionally responsive environments are not just supportive—they're essential. They reduce clinician burnout, improve patient outcomes, and increase diagnostic accuracy.

And in family systems, emotionally grounded parenting fosters co-regulation, promotes healthy attachment, and interrupts cycles of reactivity and shame.

These examples remind us that emotional capacity is not a bonus skill—it's the infrastructure of sustainable influence. It is the foundation of human flourishing across all domains—organizational, educational, clinical, and communal.

Designing Emotionally Attuned Spaces

Designing emotionally attuned spaces is not about décor—it's about emotional architecture.

It involves intentional design—of practices, policies, language, and presence—that makes safety, connection, and growth not only possible, but predictable.

This emotional architecture spans:

The physical environment—spaces arranged for inclusion, reflection, conversation, and calm.

Relational norms—how people engage, how conflict is addressed, and whether vulnerability is welcomed or dismissed.

Modeling from those in roles of influence—where empathy, curiosity, and emotional regulation replace control, reactivity, or performance.

True leadership is not about commanding a room.

It's about shaping one—so that others feel safe enough to show up fully.

Systems and policies should promote healthy emotional expression, not penalize it. And cultural responsiveness must be woven into design—honoring diverse communication styles and emotional needs rather than flattening them.

All of this contributes to a culture that determines whether a space is emotionally nourishing or emotionally exhausting.

Systemic Emotional Integration: Embedding Values into Structure

True emotional culture is not built on sentiment—it is built on systems. Systemic emotional integration involves embedding emotional values such as dignity, empathy, and psychological safety into the scaffolding of organizational design. This includes not only rituals of connection and feedback loops that prioritize care, but also accountability structures that reinforce emotional clarity and relational trust. When reflection is institutionalized, when feedback includes emotional impact, and when rituals like team gratitude circles or restorative pauses are normalized, a culture of emotional fluency becomes self-sustaining. These embedded elements ensure that emotional growth is not the exception but the expectation, woven into how people gather, how they work, and how they lead together.

Creating Emotionally Responsive Workspaces

Work is one of the most emotionally charged environments we inhabit. Yet traditional workplace design has often ignored emotional reality. For too long, employees have been expected to leave their feelings at the door—producing without pause, performing without processing.

That model is breaking down—and rightly so.

According to Gallup's 2023 *State of the Global Workplace Report*, only twenty-three percent of employees worldwide are engaged at work. The strongest predictor of engagement? Not compensation or praise, but whether someone at work genuinely cares about them—whether they are seen and valued.

Emotionally responsive workplaces are built on psychological safety, compassionate leadership, trauma-informed management, and restorative feedback cultures. These environments normalize open, honest communication without fear of retribution. They promote empathy and emotional regulation. And they hold people accountable in ways aligned with care and support—not humiliation.

Google's landmark Project Aristotle found that the highest-performing teams shared one consistent trait: psychological safety. It's not degrees. It's not experience. It's safety. This safety is not accidental—it must be intentionally cultivated through leader training, team norms, honest dialogue, and cultural audits. The return on investment? Teams that not only perform better but also stay longer, grow deeper, and show up with greater purpose and creativity.

Emotionally Attuned Classrooms and Learning Environments

In educational settings, the emotional climate of the classroom is just as important as the content of the curriculum. Students cannot thrive in environments where they do not feel emotionally safe. And safety involves more than discipline policies—it includes tone, expectations, and the quality of connection.

Emotionally attuned classrooms are guided by educators who recognize that behavior is communication, that equity requires emotional responsiveness, and that relationships must take precedence over rigor. These educators integrate social-emotional learning, apply culturally responsive practices, model co-regulation, and address misbehavior with curiosity and accountability rather than punishment or shame.

Studies from the Yale Center for Emotional Intelligence show that when teachers model emotional regulation, students exhibit higher levels of empathy, engagement, and academic performance. Trauma-informed classrooms have been shown to reduce behavioral incidents and enhance students' sense of school connectedness. These classrooms do not lower standards; they recognize the humanity of the students and prepare them not only for tests but also for life.

Designing Families and Communities with Emotional Depth

Home serves as our first emotional classroom. For many, it is also the place where the earliest wounds begin. Designing emotionally attuned families means raising children not only with rules, but through relationship. It requires modeling emotional honesty, validating feelings, and establishing rituals of reflection—not merely routines of achievement.

Emotionally grounded homes become safe spaces where feelings are acknowledged and normalized, mistakes are met with repair rather than shame, differences are respected, and boundaries are both clear and nurturing. This kind of emotional foundation prepares children for emotionally present relationships, inclusive classrooms, and compassionate leadership.

For adults, it offers space for healing, re-parenting, and emotional integration—the process of weaving together past experiences, inherited patterns, and present awareness into a more whole and conscious self. This integration ensures that unprocessed wounds are not passed forward as legacy, but transformed into insight, compassion, and intentional guidance.

Emotional insight transforms conflict into collaboration within community spaces. Places of worship, neighborhood coalitions, and local governments benefit from leaders who serve as emotional anchors—individuals who listen, create space for challenging conversations, and build bridges across cultural, racial, and generational divides. Emotionally attuned communities are inclusive by design—not merely by statement.

Emotional Design in the Built Environment

While much of this work is relational, we cannot overlook the built environment: the influence of architecture, layout, and spatial design on emotional experience. Biophilic design, for example, integrates nature into architecture and is associated with reduced stress, improved mood, and enhanced cognitive function.

Quiet spaces, calming color palettes, natural lighting, and inclusive accessibility features promote regulation and safety. Emotion-centered design isn't about luxury; it's about fostering conditions for wellness, dignity, and connection.

Imagine a workplace with mindfulness rooms, transparent communication hubs, and flexible seating that accommodates neurodiversity. Envision a school featuring storytelling circles, equity-focused advisory sessions, and rest periods specifically designed to acknowledge and address emotional fatigue. Visualize a city that includes benches in shaded areas, public art created for healing, and inclusive parks where everyone feels welcome. This is emotional fluency made visible.

Cultural and Generational Intelligence in Space Design

Emotionally attuned environments are not uniform. They must respond to cultural and generational differences. Some cultures prioritize communal decision-making, while others emphasize independence. Some generations were taught to suppress emotion, while others were encouraged to express it.

Designing for emotional depth means creating flexible spaces that honor both solitude and collaboration. It makes room for verbal and nonverbal expression, for tradition and innovation. And it necessitates an unwavering commitment to equity. Emotionally inclusive environments are also emotionally just. They acknowledge historical trauma, create space for grief and resistance, and center marginalized voices—not as guests, but as architects of culture.

This level of intentionality demands co-design. It requires inviting those most affected by a space to help shape it, listening attentively, asking frequently, and being open to change based on what is heard.

Sustaining an Emotionally Attuned Culture

Culture is not a one-time initiative; it is the sum of consistently practiced behaviors. Sustaining emotionally attuned spaces is not a task to check off a list—it is an ongoing investment. It requires regular reflection, leadership development rooted in emotional insight, integrated mental health support, rituals of connection, and policies that evolve in response to lived experience.

It also demands that we safeguard relational depth from dilution. Terms like *emotional fluency* can easily become corporate jargon when divorced from lived practice. A truly emotionally responsive culture is slow, intentional, and deeply human. It cannot be measured solely by key performance indicators. It must be felt—in the rhythm of relationships, in the quality of communication, in the depth of trust, and in the ability to navigate conflict with care.

The question is not merely, "Do we value emotional awareness here?" The deeper, more urgent question is: Is emotional safety the default experience for those who live, work, and learn in this space?

If not, then the design must evolve—not as a lofty aspiration, but as a moral imperative. Emotional safety and conscious leadership cannot flourish without intentional workplace design and a commitment to building cultures of presence, dignity, and care.

From Individual Change to Cultural Change

When emotional insight exists solely within an individual, it nurtures deeper connection. However, when it is embedded into a space, it cultivates a lasting sense of belonging.

We need spaces for healing, workplaces for restoration, schools for nurturing, families for breathing, and communities for caring. We need environments where emotional well-being is not left to chance but is thoughtfully designed with wisdom, equity, and love, valuing each person's unique emotional needs.

Spaces infused with emotional presence don't just affect mood—they awaken identity, possibility, and the quiet belief that transformation is within reach.

Insights from Redefining Our Spaces

One of the most overlooked aspects of emotional depth is how we relate to our physical environments. The spaces we inhabit—at home, at work, and in between—shape our nervous systems, clarity, and creativity. But what happens when those spaces no longer reflect who we are growing into?

In truth, much of the world outside our homes is beyond our control. Offices, airports, hotel rooms, conference halls, and institutions are often designed without emotional safety in mind. And yet, despite the limited influence we may have over public or professional environments, there remains one sacred space we can reclaim: the places that restore us.

Living internationally and traveling extensively has taught me this lesson in a profoundly personal way. The concept of "home" became more fluid—less about location and more about what felt emotionally safe and spiritually grounded. Whether I was in a cozy apartment in the Middle East or a guest room in a tranquil African village, I had to learn how to create an emotional sanctuary in unfamiliar spaces.

These experiences shifted my understanding of home—not as a fixed destination, but as an intentional expression of identity in motion. They helped me recognize that emotionally attuned spaces are not defined by ideal conditions—they are defined by alignment. These are spaces that make room for the version of yourself that needs to breathe, reset, and rise again.

For some, this resembles a minimalist approach—not for aesthetic trends, but as a conscious choice to reduce noise, release emotional clutter, and simplify life to create space for clarity. For others, it may involve letting go of heirlooms or old designs that were once significant but now feel like emotional burdens tied to a past phase of life.

What worked in one generation—or even one phase of your own life—might need to evolve. The objects, layouts, or rituals that once provided you comfort may now limit your creativity or drain your emotional energy.

Redefining your space isn't about rejection; it's about reinvention. It honors where you've been while choosing what genuinely supports where you're headed.

And yes, that means giving yourself permission to reimagine what healing, calm, and safety look like in your environment. It means allowing your physical space to evolve alongside your emotional maturity. It signifies that decluttering is an emotional process, and design is not just aesthetic—it is profoundly personal.

An emotionally attuned space reflects more than your style—it mirrors your values, honors your needs, protects your boundaries, and supports your intentions. It is a place where you remember who you are and make space to become who you are meant to be.

DESIGNING EMOTIONALLY RESPONSIVE SPACES

The spaces we inhabit—physically and emotionally—can either nurture our growth or reinforce disconnection. These prompts invite you to reflect on how your surroundings express your emotional values and how you might reshape them to foster greater safety, connection, and care:

- Which space in your life—home, work, or community—most reflects your emotional values? Which space feels misaligned, and why?
- Where do you feel emotionally safe to grow, stumble, or simply exist as you are? How might that sense of safety be recreated or expanded into other environments?
- What small rituals, sensory elements, or relational practices could you introduce to foster emotional depth in the spaces you live and lead?
- What does an emotionally inclusive environment look like in your home, team, or community—and how can you design for it intentionally?

You don't just design environments—you shape the emotional tone people carry within them.

CHAPTER 16

Emotional Literacy and Creativity: Finding Your Creative Voice

There is a myth that creativity requires calm. That it arrives when the world quiets, when pressure lifts, when the environment is ideal. But history—and human experience—suggests otherwise. Creativity often emerges not in ease, but in disruption. Not in comfort, but in tension. In truth, some of the most important expressions of art, storytelling, innovation, and leadership are born in times of change, when traditional language fails and something deeper must speak.

Creativity is not reserved for artists or visionaries; it is a human necessity. It is how we name what feels unspeakable, how we reclaim clarity when life feels chaotic, and how we bring our inner world into conversation with the outer one. And like emotional fluency, creativity thrives when we are present, aware, and connected to our emotional truth.

Emotional literacy becomes essential to creativity not because it makes us more productive, but because it makes us more whole. It helps us tune into our inner landscape while staying rooted in self, exploring vulnerability through courage, and embracing authenticity with compassion. In an age where performance is often valued over authenticity, emotional insight returns us to the place where creativity begins: the self.

Creativity as Emotional Integration

Creativity is often misunderstood as a talent—something you either have or do not. However, in reality, it is an emotional process. To create anything meaningful—whether it's a lesson plan, a product, a painting, or a vision—you must engage with emotions such as fear, wonder, grief, hope, doubt, and joy. These feelings are not distractions from the work; they are the work. The more you understand them, the more clearly your voice can emerge.

When we suppress emotion, we silence our creative voice. When we stay emotionally disconnected, we often default to imitation or perfectionism, creating what we think will be accepted rather than what is truly ours. Emotional fluency invites us to notice what we feel and use it—not as raw material to control, but as insight to shape. In this way, creativity becomes not only expression, but healing.

The Inner Critic and Emotional Regulation

Every creative person knows the voice of the inner critic. It is the voice that says, "This isn't good enough." "Who do you think you are?" "You should already have the answer." That voice does not originate in logic—it originates in fear. Fear of judgment, fear of exposure, fear of failure.

Emotional capacity doesn't silence the inner critic entirely, but it helps us regulate its influence. It teaches us to recognize the critic's voice as part of our survival instinct—trying to keep us safe—but not necessarily trying to help us grow. When we engage emotional regulation practices—such as pausing before reacting, naming our emotions, or reconnecting with purpose—we move from paralysis to progress. We stop waiting for flawlessness and start trusting process.

In creative work, this is everything. Because the goal is not idealism—it is authenticity. It is truth-telling. And truth, when offered from a grounded place, always finds resonance.

Creativity After Burnout

Burnout does not only drain energy; it fractures identity. Many people who once considered themselves creative no longer do—not because they lost the ability, but because their environments trained them to ignore it. Work became mechanical. Life became survival. Emotional depletion replaced imagination.

If you are trying to create while emotionally empty, you are not broken—you are burnt out. And the path back is not pressure; it is permission.

Permission to rest.

Permission to express without explaining.

Permission to rediscover joy without needing to monetize it.

Emotional fluency offers the internal safety required to create again. It tells us that creative energy cannot be forced—but it can be invited. And sometimes, the first act of creativity is simply noticing what brings you back to life.

Leading with Creative Wholeness

Creative leadership is not about charisma, innovation, or aesthetics. It is about emotional risk-taking. The leader who leads creatively is the one willing to question the status quo, to propose something new, to trust intuition when data is incomplete, and to foster environments where others feel safe to do the same.

Emotionally attuned leaders cultivate this kind of space. They understand that creativity and psychological safety are inseparable. Where there is fear, creativity shrinks. Where there is judgment, it hides. But where there is trust, vulnerability, and emotional presence, creativity expands.

In classrooms, Educators who lead with empathy redesign their curriculum to reflect not just content, but culture. In companies, leaders grounded in self-awareness give their teams space to ideate without punishment. In communities, organizers who build through care craft new models of justice and care. These are not soft contributions—they are courageous ones. And they come from those willing to lead with emotional wholeness.

The Quiet Path to Clarity: Insights from the Road and the Trail

Some of my most significant creative breakthroughs have not occurred in meetings or brainstorming sessions—they have emerged from long rides, quiet walks, and the tranquility of nature.

As a cyclist, nature walker, and hiker, I have learned that creativity and emotional clarity often emerge when the noise fades away. Those daily escapes, whether along a winding trail or beneath an open sky, have become sacred time for me. They are not just exercises; they are forms of emotional processing. They allow me to release tension, reconnect with my thoughts, and create space for something new to emerge.

I have navigated difficult emotions while riding a bike. I have made career decisions while walking through dense trees. More than once, I returned home from a hike with a solution I did not realize I was seeking. Even this book—this whole work of emotional reflection and leadership—was born from one of those moments of silence, when clarity caught up with me in motion.

There is something about movement that mirrors emotional flow. When the body is in rhythm, the mind opens up. Ideas begin to breathe. Emotions untangle. And the heart finally has room to speak.

In those moments, I am reminded that creativity does not always arise from effort—it often emerges from space, from allowing ourselves to step away from the screen, the noise, and the expectations. It comes when we stop forcing answers and allow ourselves to simply be—with nature, with spirit, with our own breath.

I now treasure those long rides and walks not only as rhythms of self-care but as sacred parts of my creative process. They've shown me that emotional attunement is not merely noticing your emotions—but allowing them the stillness they need to be understood.

It is in those quiet, internal moments that some of my most significant decisions are made—not under pressure but in peace.

Reclaiming Joy Through Creative Expression

Creativity is also a source of joy—not happiness tied to outcomes, but joy that arises in the moment itself. In that state, your nervous system relaxes, your thoughts quiet, and you become fully immersed in the present.

When we create, we lean into a joy that doesn't depend on approval. It is joy for its own sake, rooted in mindful engagement. In a world shaped by grief and grind, this kind of joy is revolutionary.

Emotionally present individuals allow themselves to play, try, laugh, and explore. They make time for creative expression—even if it never earns "likes" or generates revenue. They recognize that creative joy is medicine—for themselves and for others.

Your creativity does not need to be monetized to matter; it simply needs to be experienced.

Creativity as a Form of Healing

Ultimately, creativity is one of the most powerful tools for healing. Journaling, painting, dancing, composing, cooking, and designing are all ways of processing emotions that words alone cannot hold.

Therapeutic studies have shown that creative expression is not just a tool—it is a transformative force. It reduces cortisol levels, aids in trauma recovery, and strengthens emotional regulation. It gives shape to what feels formless, externalizes pain, and creates a pathway for both healing and growth.

If you are carrying grief, consider writing about it in a journal or through poetry. If you are feeling anger, move it through your body with dance or physical activity. If you feel joy, share it through music or art. And if you have a story to tell, tell it—even if your voice shakes.

Emotionally attuned creativity transcends beauty—it embodies truth. And when truth is expressed through art, it liberates us.

The World Needs Your Voice

If you have spent years stifling your creativity, doubting your voice, or waiting for permission, let this be the moment you reclaim it. You were born to create—not because you have something to prove, but because you have something to express.

Your emotions are not barriers to your creativity; they are invitations. They serve as access points to your most authentic ideas, stories, and solutions. When you create from that space, you don't just make something new; you transform into someone new.

The world doesn't need more perfect work; it needs more honest voices. And your voice—your creative, emotional, evolving voice—is needed now more than ever.

So go ahead and create anyway.

Reflection

EMOTIONAL LITERACY AND CREATIVITY: FINDING YOUR CREATIVE VOICE

Creativity thrives in environments where emotions are welcomed—not suppressed. These prompts invite you to explore how your inner emotional landscape shapes your ability to create, innovate, and imagine. Whether you're building something artistic, relational, or professional, your creative voice reflects your emotional freedom.

- When was the last time you gave yourself full permission to create without judgment, and what did you discover about yourself in the process?
- What emotions tend to arise when you approach something new, unpolished, or unfamiliar—and how do you typically respond to them?
- Where in your life or leadership could you create more space for wonder, experimentation, and emotional expression?
- How can your creative expression be used to affirm the dignity, stories, and emotional truths of communities beyond your own?

*Your creativity doesn't need to be perfect.
It needs to be honest.*

CHAPTER 17

Global Emotional Fluency — Building Relationships Across Borders

In a world that feels both more connected and more fragmented, emotional fluency must extend beyond individual experiences. It must evolve into something global, transcending language, crossing time zones, and acknowledging that our feelings, expressions, and connections are often shaped by culture as much as by character.

This kind of awareness is not just a topic for discussion—it is essential, especially in leadership. It plays a vital role in diverse teams, international schools, cross-border projects, and multicultural communities. It is not an optional add-on; it is a fundamental requirement for effective leadership.

Global emotional fluency encourages us to move beyond surface-level awareness. At its core is emotional resonance—the capacity to sense and respond to emotional cues across cultural lines with depth and humility. It urges us to understand how emotions are expressed, interpreted, and honored across different contexts. Emotional resonance allows us to substitute assumptions with inquiry, control with curiosity, and authority with deep listening—creating space for mutual respect and genuine connection.

My experiences in different countries were not merely moments; they were transformative encounters that reshaped my understanding of cross-cultural empathy and interpersonal depth. They focused not on evaluating systems or judging cultural norms, but on deeply and respectfully understanding—without assumptions—how people care, connect, and lead.

As a guest in each of these countries, I recognized that I was entering something established long before my arrival. I did not view these differences as contrasts to the West, but rather as complete and unified expressions of how people care, connect, and lead. I held a deep respect for these cultural nuances, understanding that they are essential for fostering global relationships.

What follows are not observations from an outsider looking in, but reflections from someone who was welcomed, included, and deeply affected by what I witnessed and received.

Lessons from China: Respect Moves Slower Than Words

In China, I found myself immersed in an unhurried rhythm. Meetings unfolded like ceremonies—greeted with tea, accompanied by thoughtful silence, and carried by a dignity I had not experienced before. There was beauty in the restraint, the pauses between words, and silence that was not empty but expectant. I noticed that respect was not just spoken but lived. Every interaction felt like an offering, a gesture full of meaning. Feedback did not come quickly, but when it did, it arrived with intentionality and care.

Being in those rooms taught me the value of tuning into the emotional undercurrent, valuing what was unsaid more than what was spoken. In this space, I learned to slow down and match the rhythm of the room, experiencing a genuine connection that required neither applause nor affirmation. It was mutual regard, steeped in grace.

Lessons from India: The Power of Generosity in Connection

India welcomed me with open arms, and every moment there reminded me that emotional fluency is not always loud; it is expressed through gestures. I was greeted not with urgency but with tea, a warm smile, a tilak gently placed on my forehead, and often a small gift or offering of food. Sometimes, after formal discussions, there would be sandwiches, extended conversations, and small tokens of appreciation—acts that felt deeply personal and incredibly humbling.

This was not a formality; it was a cultural expression. It conveyed that I was not just participating in a meeting—I was being received, honored, and welcomed into something communal. In India, emotional hospitality is sacred and inseparable from the task; it is the task. Attunement is valued, and connection is something to cherish, not rush through.

India taught me to slow down, to truly embrace kindness, and to understand that in some places, relational intelligence is measured not by what you say, but by how fully you are willing to be with others.

Lessons from South Africa: Beauty and Complexity Intertwined

South Africa stretched me in ways I did not expect. The land was breathtaking—mountains, coastlines, and skies made me feel both small and whole. Yet beneath the beauty lay pain, a history echoing in the present. As a guest, I felt welcomed and was aware that I was standing on sacred, scarred ground. The racial divide was real, and the emotional residue of apartheid was palpable. While I may not have fully experienced the depth of this reality, I could feel it—especially in spaces where heritage and healing intertwined.

There was no speech or formal introduction at one gathering, only a cultural dance. Rhythmic. Rooted. Radiant. The women moved with power, memory, and ancestral strength in every step. No words were spoken, but so much was conveyed. I stood in awe of the movement and the message: We are still here. We remember. We rise. This moment instilled in me a profound respect for the power of nonverbal communication and the rich cultural heritage of South Africa.

This moment reminded me that psychological wholeness encompasses the nonverbal, the embodied, and the historical. You cannot always speak healing into existence—sometimes, it must be danced, witnessed, or simply held. South Africa taught me that the body remembers, and occasionally, the most profound emotional truths are expressed in silence, movement, and collective rhythm. Emotional awareness is not always neat or polished; at times, it can be messy. But it is also sacred.

Lessons from Spain: Complete Presence Without Apology

My experience with Spain began long before I actually arrived in the country. I worked with a colleague from Spain and noticed something different from the very beginning. He embodied emotional openness. His energy was felt before he ever spoke a word. He expressed his emotions with honesty and transparency, never hiding behind a professional facade. Whether he felt moved or disappointed, you could tell. There was strength in it; it was not overbearing but rather sincere.

When I finally visited Spain, I immersed myself in the culture: the long meals, the laughter echoing through the alleyways, and the unhurried conversations. It felt like a society that still prioritizes being over doing. In the stillness, in the shared emotional space, I was reminded that emotional resilience sometimes means allowing the moment to be fully felt—and shared.

Lessons from Uganda: Legacy Woven in Respect

Uganda welcomed me not with haste, but with heritage. From the moment I arrived, I was enveloped in a quiet strength—a sense that identity here was not constructed but inherited. Elders were not merely respected; they were honored as living libraries of wisdom. Greetings were offered with both hands, not just out of politeness but as a sacred act of cultural integrity.

In Uganda, family is everything—broad, extended, and fiercely connected. It is where identity is formed, values are taught, and love is expressed through care, emotional availability, and duty. The emotional current within families runs deep, often unspoken, yet undeniably strong. Roles between men and women tend to be traditional, yet are carried out with mutual dignity. I witnessed women leading with gentleness and strength, and men speaking with humility and protection—each upholding their role in a delicate, emotional choreography.

What moved me most was not only observing this depth of connection but also being invited into it. Entry into a Ugandan family is not assumed; it must be extended by someone already within. I was embraced as a sister—not as a visitor, nor as a guest, but as kin. Such a welcome is a profound emotional gesture, one that carries weight. To be invited in is to be trusted, to be seen, and to be folded into a lineage that values belonging over performance.

I was equally inspired by the stories of those who had left and returned. Ugandan expatriates, after years abroad, came home not only to visit but also to build. Their return was more than a relocation; it was a restoration. They returned with knowledge and a renewed reverence for the culture that raised them. Their emotional attunement was multi-layered—not only embodying global understanding but also demonstrating a profound respect for the soil that still held their name.

Uganda taught me that emotional depth is a legacy in motion. It is the respect you offer without seeking praise, the care passed down through generations, and the choice to return—not out of obligation, but because something sacred calls you back. In that return, there is healing, pride, and the quiet honoring of home.

Lessons from Egypt: Stillness Beneath the Shifting Sands

Egypt carries history like breath—quiet, powerful, and ever-present. Beneath the political unrest and modern noise, an ancient rhythm continues to hum among the people, the streets, and the land. You can feel it in the sandstone ruins, in the call to prayer echoing through Cairo's alleyways, and in the way elders speak—with memory, not merely opinion.

Despite occasional tensions simmering beneath the surface, I discovered a profound gentleness among the people. Strangers offered kindness without hesitation, seeing me not as an outsider but as someone who belonged—an extension of their community. Their emotional depth was subtle yet undeniable. It resided in laughter shared across generations, in the quiet protection offered by elders, and in the graciousness found even in the simplest encounters. In a place often marked by its history and unrest, it was the people's softness that left the deepest impression.

Cultural dances also conveyed stories without words. Whether during a Nubian celebration or a Sufi performance, I felt a profound connection—where movement replaced speech and joy became a collective experience. These rituals required no translation; they spoke a universal language of spirit, resilience, and joy.

Egypt taught me that emotional resilience is not always forged in ease. Sometimes, it is shaped through hardship and passed down like an heirloom. In a place where beauty and struggle coexist, kindness becomes a deliberate choice, and grounded stillness becomes a form of protest against chaos. Egypt reminded me that when the world around you is uncertain, your ability to remain generous, joyful, and grounded represents a unique form of leadership.

This Is What Shapes Us

These experiences did more than expose me to various ways of working and communicating; they unveiled the emotional core of cultures I had previously studied from afar. They reminded me of something fundamental: emotional literacy is not universally expressed—but it is universally vital, connecting us all in our shared humanity.

I did not enter these spaces to analyze or evaluate the structure of emotional hierarchies; that is not my role. I entered as a guest, and in doing so, I was gifted something profound. I observed how each culture extends care, honors tradition, and cultivates emotional attunement in its own way.

Some express it through ceremony, while others do so through silence; some through openness, and others through restraint. None of these approaches are right or wrong. They are simply different, and beautifully so.

Cultural-emotional depth asks not for judgment of our differences, but for reverence. It calls us to show up with presence, humility, and the awareness that every interaction carries layers of unseen history, identity, and meaning. So, wherever you go, may you carry that lens with you—not one of critique but of curiosity, not of comparison but of connection, fostering a sense of open-mindedness and respect for cultural diversity.

Because true emotional depth is not just about how much you know—it is about how well you listen, how deeply you see, and how humbly you receive.

Global Emotional Attunement: The Bridge Connecting Us

These experiences, each unique and deeply human, taught me that emotional awareness is not confined to a single culture, language, or leadership style. It is vast and evolving, expressed in gestures, silences, and subtleties that remain invisible to the untrained eye.

Emotional literacy may be a universal language, but it speaks in many dialects. It is not enough to be relationally attuned within our own cultural norms; we must become emotionally adaptable to others. We must recognize that what is viewed as confident in one space may seem aggressive in another. What signals respect in one region may feel distant in another. The most insightful questions we can ask are: "How do you feel seen? How do you feel safe?"

To lead with global emotional attunement is to release the belief that our way is the only way. It means listening to nuance before offering certainty, reflecting on our own conditioning before interpreting the actions of others, and learning from people—not just about them.

It is the art of embracing difference with openness and compassion. It reminds us that leadership is not only about direction—it is about understanding. Not just across geographies, but across experiences, perspectives, and identities.

In a world increasingly defined by division, this capacity is what brings us back to one another. It is the bridge that holds us together.

So wherever you go—whether crossing cultural lines or sitting across from someone whose worldview challenges your own—may you carry your emotional attunement like a passport: open, prepared, stamped with humility, and fluent in compassion.

At the end of the day, regardless of origin or identity, we all long for the same things: to feel safe, to be understood, and to truly connect.

Reflection

GLOBAL EMOTIONAL FLUENCY — BUILDING RELATIONSHIPS ACROSS BORDERS

True connection across cultures begins with emotional humility. These prompts encourage you to reflect on how your worldview has been shaped by global encounters—and how emotional fluency can help you build trust, challenge assumptions, and evolve without losing yourself in the process.

- What cultural assumptions have you had to unlearn in order to build more authentic relationships across difference?
- When have you witnessed emotional awareness bridge a cultural or generational gap—and what did you learn from that moment?
- How do you remain rooted in your identity while remaining open to transformation through global connection?
- How do you maintain emotional clarity while navigating cross-cultural relationships or global teams?

Global emotional fluency is not about fitting in everywhere— it's about showing up fully while honoring difference.

Global Presence: Identity, Belonging, and Cultural Attunement

You are not just one story.
You are a mosaic made up of memories, voices, cultures,
and the process of becoming.

Do not shrink to fit a single frame.
Do not erase yourself to belong.

You can embrace many truths.
You can lead through differences.
You can rise fully.

The world needs all of you—
not just the aspects that are easy to explain.

PART V

IDENTITY, BELONGING, AND EMOTIONAL ATTUNEMENT IN A GLOBAL WORLD

Our identities are layered, and our sense of belonging is often tested—especially in a globalized world where cultures, roles, and expectations constantly evolve. This section explores how emotional depth can serve as a compass for navigating difference, bridging across cultural divides, and reconstructing the self in complex social landscapes. These reflections lay the emotional groundwork for what comes next: a transformative framework that brings these lessons into practice.

CHAPTER 18

Emotional Attunement and Identity Formation in a Global Context

Identity is not a fixed destination; it is a living mosaic—shaped by every culture we encounter, every story we inherit, and every moment we choose to evolve. As *emotional literacy* helps us lead and relate to others, it also guides us inward—toward understanding the personal narratives we carry across time and space.

This chapter builds on the foundation of global emotional attunement by turning inward. It examines how our sense of self is formed, disrupted, and redefined through cross-cultural experiences, internal conflict, and the quiet labor of growth. Here, identity is not simply a label—it is a lifelong journey of alignment, reflection, and becoming.

Living, working, or leading in cross-cultural contexts accelerates the journey of identity formation. Whether we are educators, consultants, business leaders, or creatives, entering a new environment often disrupts how we perceive ourselves and others. What once felt certain becomes complex; what was once assumed is questioned. Amid this transformation, relational intelligence helps us stay grounded in our values while remaining open to growth. It enables leaders to embrace difference without losing their voice—to navigate global spaces with humility, presence, and emotional clarity. It is the capacity to honor diversity while remaining anchored in self—bridging cultural boundaries without abandoning identity.

The Fluidity of Identity

Identity is not a static label; it is a living, breathing collection of beliefs, affiliations, values, and self-perceptions that evolve over time. According to social identity theory, our sense of self is shaped by the groups to which we belong—both socially and psychologically. We define ourselves through nationality, race, profession, gender, and social affiliations. However, when we transition between cultural contexts, these identity markers are not always understood or valued in the same way.

In my doctoral research, I examined the identity development of Western teachers working in the United Arab Emirates. What emerged was a compelling portrait of how emotional attunement influences one's ability to adapt, reflect, and remain authentic while navigating unfamiliar cultural terrain. Teachers continuously interpreted and reinterpreted their sense of self in an environment where their identity was both visible and invisible. Their experiences provide insight into how identity formation is profoundly emotional and socially negotiated.

Inner Awareness in Constructing Identity

One of the foundational pillars of emotional depth is inner awareness. In global contexts, this involves more than just recognizing your strengths and weaknesses; it also encompasses the ability to observe how your identity is reshaped by cultural tension, differences, and dissonance.

Many participants in the study described an initial shock upon arriving in the UAE—not just culture shock in the traditional sense, but an internal conflict about their identities in this new environment. Some expressed feelings of being misunderstood, while others felt a strong urge to assimilate or retreat. Social categorization and social comparison became key tools for understanding their place. Participants noted how in-group and out-group dynamics formed quickly, often based on shared nationality, language, or values. This created a perceived hierarchy of belonging—and for many, a question: where do I truly belong?

Emotional literacy enables us to answer this question with honesty and grace. Self-aware individuals do not deny these tensions; rather, they explore them. They ask, "Why am I reacting this way?" "What do I need in this moment?" "How can I remain authentic while honoring differences?" This internal dialogue fosters growth and allows identity to evolve without collapsing.

Emotional Attunement and Cultural Humility

Another core dimension of emotional attunement is the capacity to understand and share in the emotional experiences of others. In cross-cultural settings, this ability evolves into cultural humility—a posture of curiosity, the willingness to learn without defensiveness, and the recognition that your way is not the only way.

The Western teachers in my study often expressed frustration when their educational practices or leadership styles were misunderstood. However, those who embraced attunement began to shift their perspective. They asked deeper questions about the cultural values influencing certain behaviors. They became less reactive and more reflective. They recognized that emotional presence was not about fitting in or standing out—it was about engaging in ways that honored cultural context.

Relational insight allows us to suspend judgment and remain curious. When our sense of identity feels challenged, attunement reminds us that our perspective is one among many. It invites us into connection—even when the terrain is unfamiliar.

Social Awareness and Emotional Connection

Social awareness is the ability to read the room—perceiving social dynamics, cultural norms, and emotional energy. It becomes particularly important when our identity is neither mirrored nor affirmed by our environment.

Participants in the study described how the secondary school environment in the UAE played a crucial role in their identity development. When the environment was emotionally supportive and inclusive, identity formation was fluid and empowering. In contrast, when it was rigid or dismissive, identity became a source of struggle. Teachers emphasized the significance of community, safe spaces, and meaningful connections—not only in a professional context but also personally.

This reflects a fundamental truth: identity is not formed in isolation—it is shaped through relationships. Understanding our emotions helps us connect more deeply, recognize when we feel safe, notice how stress influences our behavior, and know when to advocate for our emotional well-being.

It also empowers us to create emotionally attuned environments for others—spaces where identity can be explored without fear of judgment, shame, or exclusion.

The Courage to Evolve

Perhaps the most powerful lesson from this research is that evolving identity requires courage. It demands a willingness to relinquish certainty, embrace change, and inhabit the space between who you were and who you are becoming. Emotional attunement provides the scaffolding for this transformation. It teaches us to navigate ambiguity with compassion, guide ourselves through discomfort, and extract meaning from experiences that challenge our self-perception.

Identity development in global spaces is not merely a personal journey—it is a leadership practice. Whether you are an educator in an international classroom, a consultant in a cross-border firm, or a student navigating cultural complexity, your ability to manage your emotions, remain anchored in your values, and build bridges across difference is your greatest strength.

The world is shifting. Cultures are intersecting. Through it all, emotional resilience allows our identities to expand rather than fracture. When we understand who we are—and have the internal tools to stay grounded—we enter new environments not as outsiders, but as contributors and leaders.

Reflection

EMOTIONAL ATTUNEMENT AND IDENTITY FORMATION IN A GLOBAL CONTEXT

Identity is not fixed—it is lived, layered, and reshaped by every border we cross, both literal and emotional. These prompts invite you to explore how emotional depth has helped you navigate belonging, loss, conflict, and clarity in the context of global identity. When your world expands, so does your understanding of yourself.

- How has living or working in a different cultural environment challenged or expanded your understanding of who you are?
- What parts of your identity have felt most misunderstood—and how have you learned to honor them with emotional integrity?
- In what ways has emotional literacy helped you reconcile the tension between belonging and evolving?
- How has emotional attunement helped you recognize—and shift—biases that impact how you view and value cultural difference?

Your identity is not a destination—it is a mosaic shaped by emotion, connection, and choice.

CHAPTER 19

The Conflict of Belonging — Navigating Social Identity Across Cultures

Belonging is both a longing and a battleground. It is the invisible thread we seek to hold, even when it frays under cultural tension or social exclusion. Following our exploration of identity development, this chapter dives deeper into the emotional turbulence that emerges when belonging feels conditional. Through the lens of emotional attunement, we'll examine how people navigate the tension between fitting in and remaining whole—and how we reclaim our sense of self across borders and expectations.

In global environments, we often find ourselves caught in a complex dance between connection and exclusion. We are invited to the table, but not always welcomed into the conversation. We are visible, yet not always valued. And from that tension, a quiet conflict emerges—the conflict of belonging.

Emotional depth becomes essential for naming, navigating, and healing this often invisible experience. It allows us to recognize the emotional cost of assimilation, the pain of erasure, and the strength required to stay rooted in who we are while adapting to where we are.

Understanding the Layers of Belonging

Belonging is not binary; it exists in layers and is influenced by multiple factors—cultural familiarity, shared values, language, power dynamics, and perceived differences. In cross-cultural settings, these layers become even more pronounced. We are not only seeking to belong as individuals; we are also striving to belong as representatives of specific backgrounds, worldviews, or identity markers.

In my research with Western educators working in the UAE, participants expressed that although they were professionally positioned on international teams, they did not always experience emotional inclusion. Many described feeling like cultural outsiders despite their qualifications and commitment. They developed amicable relationships with out-group colleagues but noted a clear boundary between those interactions and the deeper emotional connections formed within their in-group—often based on shared cultural norms or nationality.

This highlights the often painful truth that the hope for intercultural acceptance is frequently undermined by persistent stereotypes, stigma, and social distance. People long to be accepted for who they are; however, in diverse environments, belonging is often earned conditionally rather than freely granted.

The Emotional Toll of Social Navigation

Emotional resonance, particularly self-regulation and social awareness, was essential in these situations. Those who cultivated emotional stamina were better equipped to manage their internal dissonance and choose responses that aligned with both their values and the cultural context. For individuals navigating diverse cultural environments, there is often a continuous emotional calculation. Should I speak up or remain silent? Should I assert my perspective or defer? Will my voice be welcomed or critiqued? Over time, these choices can lead to emotional fatigue.

The Western educators in my study noted that much of their energy was devoted to interpreting social cues and adjusting their behaviors to maintain surface harmony. While this approach protected them from overt conflict, it also limited authentic engagement. Emotional resonance, particularly self-regulation and social awareness, was essential in these situations. Those who cultivated emotional stamina were better equipped to manage their internal dissonance and choose responses that aligned with both their values and the cultural context.

However, even with emotional skills, the absence of true belonging took its toll. Participants described the burden of not being fully known or understood. Over time, many compartmentalized their school and personal lives—not out of avoidance, but as a form of self-protection. This fragmented identity represents a subtle form of survival—one that emotionally attuned leaders must learn to recognize and compassionately address.

Belonging and the Importance of Emotional Safety

Psychological safety is one of the most significant contributors to a sense of belonging. When individuals feel free to express themselves without fear of judgment or retaliation, they are more likely to engage, contribute, and lead. But when emotional safety is compromised, people tend to shrink. They self-censor, withdraw, or overcompensate.

Creating cultures of emotional safety requires more than policies or training—it demands modeling. Leaders must demonstrate curiosity, compassion, and courage. They need to recognize bias, name cultural blind spots, and extend empathy across difference. Emotional resonance becomes the bridge, prompting leaders to ask:

"Who is not speaking?"

"Who is not being seen?"

"Who is silently adjusting just to survive?"

In emotionally responsive environments, diversity is not a checkbox—it is a core value. Cultural differences are not inconveniences; they are insights. Through this shift, belonging becomes not just possible—but expected. And not only for those in the majority—for everyone.

Selective Engagement: A Response to Emotional Exclusion

One of the more nuanced findings of my study was the concept of selective reciprocal interaction. Participants described choosing when, how, and with whom to engage based on their previous experiences of emotional exclusion. This was not pettiness; it was wisdom gained from emotional wounds. If trust was broken, they withdrew. If curiosity was shown, they leaned in.

This subtle behavior is important. It reminds us that inclusion is not just about inviting people into the space; it also encompasses how they are treated once they arrive. People do not forget how they are made to feel, and over time, they create internal maps to avoid emotional harm. Leaders lacking emotional literacy often misinterpret this behavior as aloofness or a lack of initiative when, in reality, it often signifies self-preservation.

Redefining Belonging as an Act of Leadership

Belonging is not merely a feeling; it is shaped by how systems are structured and how leaders engage. Emotionally attuned leadership redefines belonging as an active process. It is not assumed; it is constructed. It is not passively hoped for—it is intentionally cultivated.

To lead across cultures is to continually invite new perspectives and ways of being. It is to recognize that our differences are not threats—they are gifts. It is to build environments where people feel free to express their identities without fear of rejection. And it is to listen deeply enough to perceive the silent conflict of those who are present in body, but hidden in spirit.

We cannot assume that a smile means someone feels seen. Contribution does not always equate to connection. Emotional resonance teaches us to look beneath the surface—to recognize when someone is participating outwardly but disconnected inwardly. It is the resonance between presence and perception that reveals whether belonging is genuine or performative.

Reflection

THE CONFLICT OF BELONGING — NAVIGATING SOCIAL IDENTITY ACROSS CULTURES

Belonging isn't always about acceptance—it's about feeling seen without having to disappear. These prompts invite you to reflect on the emotional tension of holding your identity in spaces that may misinterpret, challenge, or marginalize it. Emotional depth helps you discern when to adapt, when to advocate, and when to stay grounded in who you are.

- When have you felt like an outsider in a space that was supposed to feel familiar—and how did you respond emotionally?
- What strategies have helped you maintain self-awareness and self-worth when your identity was misread or marginalized?
- How do you discern when to adapt, when to advocate, and when to walk away in order to protect your emotional alignment?
- Where have you felt "in between" or "outside"—and how can those experiences help you lead with deeper empathy toward others navigating identity conflict?
- How can your own journey of identity and belonging help you lead with more compassion and authenticity?

Belonging without emotional compromise is one of the highest forms of self-respect.

CHAPTER 20

Reconstructing the Self — Leadership, Culture, and Emotional Integration

When disruption meets identity, something new is born. Often, it is not destruction—but reconstruction. This chapter concludes Part V by exploring how emotionally anchored leaders rebuild themselves after fragmentation—not by returning to what was, but by integrating all they have become.

If the previous chapters unpack how identity and belonging are challenged across cultures, this chapter offers a blueprint for emotional integration—where lived experience becomes wisdom, and inner clarity becomes leadership.

The Emotional Impact of Cultural Displacement

An identity crisis often begins quietly. It is not always the result of trauma or sudden change. More often, it is a gradual erosion of certainty. The phrases that once defined us no longer fit. The roles that once gave us purpose feel hollow. The communities we once relied on begin to shift, and we find ourselves between worlds—not quite where we were, not quite where we are going.

In my research with Western educators in the United Arab Emirates, the identity crisis was not rooted in failure; rather, it stemmed from emotional dissonance. Participants shared how their sense of leadership and expertise was often met with indifference or resistance. Some found themselves in environments where their professional experience did not culturally translate. Others struggled with isolation, feeling unseen or misunderstood. Over time, this disconnect triggered a profound reevaluation of self.

What they experienced is not unique to educators; it reflects the emotional toll of cultural displacement. However, this dissonance can serve as the birthplace of transformation.

From Disassociation to Integration

Reconstructing identity begins with emotional integration—the process of reconciling our past selves with our evolving sense of who we are becoming. In emotionally attuned leadership, this journey requires honesty, humility, and a willingness to be transformed by experience.

Several participants in my study described experiencing periods of disassociation—a desire to emotionally detach from their environment in order to preserve a sense of self. This is a natural protective response. Yet those who experienced the most meaningful growth were the ones who moved beyond disconnection and toward wholeness. They began asking:

What parts of my identity still serve me?

What parts need to evolve?

How can I remain anchored in my values while expanding my cultural understanding?

This inner work is demanding—but essential.

Those rooted in emotional integrity understand that real transformation begins with emotional integration—the ability to reconcile the fragmented parts of self into a coherent whole. Without integration, influence becomes performative. With it, guidance becomes embodied.

The ability to support others through ambiguity is directly shaped by how we metabolize our own experiences—transforming them into wisdom, steadiness, and presence.

Leadership as Identity Development

In multicultural environments, leadership is not just functional—it is formational.

It becomes a dimension of identity work.

To lead well in these spaces, we must draw not only from our professional expertise but from our evolving humanity. This was evident in my study of Western educators navigating cross-cultural roles. When they were invited—formally or informally—into positions of guidance, something shifted. Their sense of purpose deepened. Those asked to lead content areas, mentor peers, or shape curriculum described a surprising outcome: they felt reintegrated into their professional identities.

In these moments, leadership was not about hierarchy.

It was about being seen.

Transformational leadership theory reminds us that the most effective leaders uplift those around them. But the reverse is also true: transformational environments uplift the leader. When we are trusted, we thrive. When we are acknowledged, we grow. And when we are given room to contribute authentically, we become more ourselves.

By contrast, in contexts where influence was neither encouraged nor recognized, participants described a quiet disengagement. They continued to perform—but their emotional investment waned. Over time, they became distant from their own potential.

This reveals a deeper truth:

When identity is not valued, presence becomes muted.

People may remain—but they will not flourish.

Dr. Karissa Thomas

The Role of Emotional Attunement in Rebuilding Identity

Emotional attunement offers the tools to reconstruct identity with integrity. Grounded awareness enables us to notice when our inner world no longer aligns with our external environment. Emotional regulation allows us to respond thoughtfully rather than react impulsively. Empathy creates space to hold the discomfort of others while managing our own. And relational literacy equips us to read the room—with clarity, care, and cultural sensitivity.

As our identity evolves, these capacities become essential. We are not simply managing roles or responsibilities—we are rewriting the unfolding narrative of who we are. Emotional depth offers a framework for that transformation to be honest, intentional, and growth-oriented.

The Stories Beneath Our Stories

Many of us have traveled across countries, careers, cultures, and identities. Some journeys were chosen, while others were forced. Some began in childhood with no choice at all, while others were inherited silently, passed through bloodlines, and whispered in family myths.

We come from places that carry history—sometimes painful, sometimes proud. Colonialism, migration, displacement, war, and survival have shaped the paths of countless leaders. And while we often lead from our immediate experiences, there is a much deeper well beneath our day-to-day lives.

We are not just the stories we tell—we are also the stories we haven't yet uncovered.

When we begin to honor that deeper lineage—when we trace our emotional and ancestral roots—we unlock a power far greater than performance. We become leaders rooted in empathy. We recognize how much of the world has been uprooted, how many people are still seeking home, identity, or safety. And that recognition becomes a doorway to inclusive leadership.

So many people live at the tip of the iceberg. But when we honor the roots beneath the surface—when we pause to ask, "What ground do I truly come from?"—we surprise ourselves. Our vision expands, our compassion grows, and our ability to lead across borders, cultures, and differences deepens.

This is not about romanticizing pain—it's about honoring the mosaic of what makes us human. In doing so, we become better equipped to lead a world that is longing for connection, healing, and home.

Embracing the Questions, Guiding Through Them

Rainer Maria Rilke once wrote, "Be patient toward all that is unsolved in your heart and try to love the questions themselves." This captures the essence of identity reconstruction. It is not a quick fix, nor a linear ascent. It is the willingness to sit with inquiry: Who am I now? Who am I becoming? What matters most in this season?

Emotionally grounded leadership doesn't require having all the answers. It calls for authenticity, the courage to grow in public, and the humility to lead while still learning. It is the ability to embody emotional resilience while extending grace to others.

In global and multicultural environments, the most impactful leaders understand that identity is not static—it is fluid, responsive, and powerful. They cultivate spaces where individuals can evolve without shame. They don't just support transformation; they model it. And in doing so, they co-create organizations that are not only high-performing but also deeply human.

Identity, after all, is not a final destination—it is a living story. And emotional attunement becomes the pen with which we author it, intentionally and with care.

Reflection

RECONSTRUCTING THE SELF — LEADERSHIP, CULTURE, AND EMOTIONAL INTEGRATION

Guiding others is not a static act—it evolves with every experience, every challenge, and every reinvention of self.

As we navigate personal, cultural, and professional shifts, emotional attunement becomes the throughline that connects our internal clarity to our external impact. These prompts invite you to reflect on how your sense of influence has expanded—not just through roles or responsibilities, but through identity transformation.

At the heart of sustainable presence is integration:

Where who you are and how you show up remain in alignment.

- In what ways has your sense of self in positions of influence been reshaped by cultural, personal, or professional change?
- What parts of your former identity have you released to evolve into the guide you are becoming?
- How do you remain emotionally integrated—anchored in truth, attuned to others, and responsive with care?
- What parts of your leadership identity are evolving to include more cultural humility, emotional range, and inclusive presence?

This is the ongoing work of becoming whole.

And from that wholeness, we lead—not by title, but by presence.

Bringing Mosaic into the World

You were never meant to carry the weight of change alone.
You were meant to co-create—
to build,
to listen,
to disrupt with care.

This is not just a framework—it is a movement.
Not a tool to wield,
but a truth to live.

Let your presence make space.
Let your leadership restore what hustle tried to erase.
Let your humanity be the offering.

There is no perfect rollout,
no flawless way to begin.
Only the next brave conversation.
Only the next aligned decision.
Only the choice to show up with your full self—again and again.

You are not planting perfection.
You are planting wholeness.
And the world needs exactly that.

PART VI

THE MOSAIC WAY™ — FROM FRAGMENTED TO WHOLE

This section brings the Mosaic Intelligence Method™ to life. Through personal narratives, real-world case stories, and reflective insights, you will see how emotional integrity, cultural flexibility, and identity agility shape impactful leadership in dynamic environments. Each chapter invites you to move beyond theory—embodying wholeness not as a distant ideal, but as a grounded daily practice.

CHAPTER 21

Wholeness in Action — My Mosaic Story

Trace the personal and cultural lineage that gave rise to the Mosaic Intelligence Method™, revealing how identity, resilience, and emotional truth shaped a new way of leading.

Long before I had a framework or a language for it, I was living the early threads of emotional integrity, cultural flexibility, and identity agility.

I did not arrive at this work through theory—I arrived through living.

As a Trinidadian American Black woman, my identity was often flattened into categories that never fully captured me. Though I was born into a lineage rich with migration, culture, and meaning, the world often saw only one story: African American. But like so many of us, my story is layered.

My mother—once crowned Miss Trinidad and Tobago—walked with beauty, vision, and quiet power in a world still reverberating from the civil rights movement. She stood on the Miss World stage in England with courage and elegance, pursuing dreams that weren't designed with her in mind. From her, I learned that leadership is not about waiting for permission. It's about showing up fully, even when the space was not made for you.

Before her, my maternal grandmother walked the roads of Trinidad as a water carrier, descended from East Indian laborers brought across oceans. She never read books, but she embodied a wisdom deeper than anything I could find on a page. From her, I learned that literacy and wisdom are not the same—and that emotional depth passed through generations is its own kind of knowledge.

On my father's side, my great-grandfather was Portuguese and French; my great-grandmother, Chinese and Spanish. Somehow, their paths converged in Trinidad, though the story of how remains a mystery. That mystery is part of the mosaic I carry—unanswered, but shaping me all the same.

I was raised in a swirl of traditions: Protestant, Catholic, Baptist, Hindu, Christian. At times I wondered if I should also be celebrating Chinese New Year. Each spiritual current brought its own beauty, its own complexity. Yet, the world often asked me to choose—to simplify what was never meant to be singular.

Even as a child, I was living in complexity. My earliest years unfolded in the suburbs of Queens, New York, where my neighborhood became its own classroom. My Dominican babysitter's family lived across the street, welcoming me with warmth and rhythm. My childhood best friend's Liberian household introduced me to ceremonies, spices, and strength. On the other side, my Caucasian mentors expanded my worldview with quiet consistency and care. I didn't yet have the language for it, but each home was shaping my emotional literacy—through shared meals, modeled values, and lived stories. These were not just cultural exposures; they were foundational threads of belonging.

I was still a child when I moved to Manhattan's Upper East Side—a dramatic shift in rhythm and culture. It was there, in elite institutions and quiet drawing rooms, that I learned to decode the unspoken rules of proximity, privilege, and power. I came to understand adaptation not as fragmentation, but as fluency. That, too, was the Mosaic Intelligence Method™ in motion—long before it had a name.

Still, this is not a full memoir. It cannot contain the entire story of my becoming. This is a glimpse—a thread in a larger tapestry of trials, pivots, breakthroughs, and prayers. As I reflected in Chapter 20, so many of us have had to trim our stories to fit someone else's template. But the parts of us we were asked to cast aside are often the very parts needed to lead into the future.

The leadership the world now demands—and what future generations will require—must be emotionally honest, culturally attuned, and radically inclusive. We are living through a generational shift in consciousness. Young people are not content to conform. They want workplaces where wholeness is not punished, where values are not performative, and where leadership is not positional, but deeply personal.

Research continues to confirm what many of us have long felt: organizations that center emotional safety, cultural inclusion, and identity-responsive frameworks are not only more humane—they are more resilient, effective, and sustainable.

So I lived as many things: a New Yorker, a cultural bridge, a daughter, a seeker. But life stretched me further.

I rose through corporate ranks before transitioning into education, eventually leading across classrooms, boardrooms, and global communities. I lived and worked in the Middle East, where I deepened my understanding of cultural nuance and human connection. I traveled across Africa, Asia, Europe, and the Americas—not as a tourist, but as a learner, seeking to understand people beyond assumption. Each place offered me a new lens, a new lesson.

I earned degrees—but more importantly, I earned perspective. I became both a practitioner and a scholar, shaped by lived experience and grounded in research.

Each role added dimension, but none could define me. The world often asked me to segment my story—choose a title, a lane, a singular truth. But I've come to realize: my life was never about fitting in. It was about revealing what wholeness could look like—and daring to lead from that place, even when no model existed.

What emerged was not only my voice—it was a framework for a new kind of leadership. One rooted in emotional integrity, cultural flexibility, and identity agility.

Reflection

LEADING FROM THE MOSAIC WITHIN

Take a moment to explore how your story is already shaping the way you lead, love, and live. Pause here before continuing into the Mosaic Intelligence framework.

- What parts of your story have you been asked to hide or minimize to survive or succeed?
- Which family, cultural, or neighborhood influences shaped how you see the world—and how you lead in it?
- What would it mean to reclaim those parts as strengths rather than shadows?

Your story was never too much. It was always the foundation of your wisdom.

CHAPTER 22

The Mosaic Intelligence Method™ — A Framework for Emotional Evolution

*D*iscover *a transformative model that expands emotional intelligence through integration of culture, identity, and emotional depth.*

The Mosaic Intelligence Method™ was born not at a desk—but in the in-between spaces.

After the classroom door closed.

After the client cried.

After I asked myself again: How do I lead now?

It was also born from research—my work as a scholar-practitioner studying identity, culture, and emotional development across global contexts.

This chapter is not just a framework. It is a mirror, an invitation, and a movement. For anyone who has ever felt pressured to choose one box, one version, one truth—this is your welcome. You do not have to edit yourself to lead. You do not have to be one thing to belong.

The Mosaic Way™ is for those who live between cultures, identities, and stories. It honors the fragments, the contradictions, the sacred in-between. And it reminds us: you were never too much—you were always more than enough.

When I looked back on the patterns of my own life—and the leaders I've coached through theirs—I saw something deeper. Beneath every breakthrough was a choice to lead from wholeness, not performance. To stop shrinking. To stop performing. And to start leading from within.

Throughout this book, we've explored how emotional depth shapes our inner lives, our relationships, and our ability to lead in a fractured world. We've examined disruption, healing, identity, and the emotional capacities needed to repair what's been broken.

But we now live in a moment defined by fragmentation, contradiction, and cultural collision. The emotional skills we once viewed as advanced—self-regulation, empathy, presence—are no longer enough. We need something more integrative, more layered. Something that meets the multidimensional realities of today's leadership, belonging, and change.

This is where emotional literacy must evolve.

I call this evolution the Mosaic Intelligence Method™—a human-centered framework built on three pillars:

Emotional Integrity — Aligning what you feel, what you value, and how you show up

Cultural Flexibility — Adapting across differences without erasing your essence

Identity Agility — Leading from a self that is evolving, expansive, and rooted

These are more than ideas—they are a new emotional language for influence.
Not rooted in performance, but in presence.
Not grounded in dominance, but in restoration.
Not built on certainty, but designed for complexity.

There comes a moment when all the tools we've been given—breathing exercises, feedback frameworks, emotional regulation hacks—no longer feel like enough. We show up. We apply what we know. And still, something feels fractured—within us and within the systems we lead.

That moment is not a failure of emotional intelligence. It's a threshold. An invitation.

To deepen.

To expand.

To evolve.

This chapter introduces the Mosaic Intelligence Method™ not as a replacement for emotional intelligence, but as its natural evolution—an embodied approach for leaders navigating the now.

We manage workplaces across time zones and traditions. We raise families with hybrid identities. We lead amid competing truths, shifting cultures, and historical wounds. These times require more than traditional leadership models. They demand a new kind of intelligence—one that holds contradiction, embraces complexity, and leads with wholeness.

The Three Pillars of the Mosaic Intelligence Method™

Emotional Integrity

Emotional integrity is the foundation. It's not about being emotionally composed at all times—it's about being emotionally congruent. It signifies the alignment between what you feel, what you value, and how you present yourself.

Leaders with emotional integrity do not merely perform alignment; they embody it. They speak truthfully—even when uncertain. They acknowledge the challenges, admit what they do not know, and lead with calm, clarity, and conviction.

Emotional alignment enables individuals to be genuine. It fosters trust—not through perfection, but through presence.

Cultural Flexibility

Cultural flexibility recognizes that what one culture perceives as empathy may be regarded as intrusion in another. It is the emotional capacity to adapt—without losing your essence.

It reflects the willingness to listen before responding, to respect silence as much as speech, and to engage with difference through curiosity instead of control. It is not about assimilation, but about emotional translation—bridging values and voices while preserving your own.

Identity Agility

Today's world necessitates a broader approach to leadership.

Identity agility refers to the ability to move fluidly between roles, cultures, and emotional contexts while staying grounded in your core identity. It means holding space for multiple truths within yourself—and allowing others to do the same.

Leaders with identity agility do not compartmentalize their identities to survive. They lead as whole individuals, and in doing so, they invite others to do the same.

Together, these three pillars form the heart of the Mosaic Intelligence Method™. Emotional Integrity grounds us in truth. Cultural Flexibility helps us adapt without erasure. Identity Agility empowers us to lead as our full selves. This is not just a leadership model—it is a path to wholeness in an increasingly fragmented world.

A Fresh Perspective on Emotional Literacy

A mosaic is not made from perfect, uniform pieces; it is composed of fragments—shards of glass, broken tiles, and irregular shapes. On their own, these pieces seem incomplete, but together they create something powerful, beautiful, and whole.

So it is with us.

The Mosaic Intelligence Method™ refers to the ability to lead from a place of emotional wholeness, cultural wisdom, and the integration of identity. It expands the foundation of emotional intelligence by providing a more nuanced and inclusive perspective—one that embraces complexity rather than simplifying it.

It's not about erasing differences; it's about arranging them.

It's not about overcoming brokenness; it's about finding meaning in it.

It's not about unrealistic emotional standards; it's about emotional honesty and emotional agility.

The Mosaic Way as Inclusive Leadership in Action

Inclusive leadership is not a checkbox or initiative—it is a way of being. It is the daily embodiment of emotional courage, cultural humility, and relational presence. The Mosaic Way is not separate from this—it is the practice in action.

When you lead with emotional integrity, cultural flexibility, and identity agility, you are not simply managing tasks—you are creating space where people feel seen, respected, and safe to be fully themselves.

The Mosaic Way invites us to lead from wholeness, not performance; from shared humanity, not hierarchy. It reminds us that inclusion is not about adding diverse voices to a static system—it is about transforming the system so every voice matters.

The world is not asking for louder voices—it is asking for deeper presence. Not fixed answers, but flexible identities. Not flawless authority, but meaningful connection.

Inclusive leadership is not the byproduct of the Mosaic Intelligence Method™—it is its living expression.

Why the Mosaic Intelligence Method™ Matters Today

In my doctoral research, I examined identity dissonance among Western educators in Eastern cultural contexts. Despite their expertise, many found themselves emotionally disoriented. These were not failures of intellect; they were invitations for emotional evolution.

Traditional emotional intelligence was never intended to address the complexities of cultural diversity, historical trauma, or the nuances of identity negotiations. That's where the Mosaic Intelligence Method™ comes in. It honors the unseen effort of becoming whole in environments that require fragmentation.

It articulates what many are feeling but cannot name. It empowers us to lead—not with mastery, but with humanity.

From Fragmented to Whole

The Mosaic Intelligence Method™ cannot be mastered in a single training. It is not a checklist. It is a way of being.

It is found in the pause before reacting. In the moment you choose truth over performance. In the decision to design a meeting that makes room for silence, for reflection, for difference.

Allow your leadership to reflect that intention. Let your lived experience become your greatest emotional asset.

You are not broken. You are evolving.

This is the Mosaic Intelligence Method™.

And it represents the future of emotionally fluent leadership.

Each chapter before this—on resilience, empathy, disruption, parenting, and identity—has led us to this threshold. They've offered us the tools. The Mosaic Intelligence Method™ offers us the language to integrate them. What was once fragmented becomes whole.

Reflection

LEADING WITH MOSAIC AWARENESS

Take a moment to internalize the Mosaic framework before stepping into the next chapter.

- Which pillar of the Mosaic Intelligence Method™ do you currently lead from most naturally?
- Where do you feel challenged to grow—emotionally, culturally, or in your evolving identity?
- What might shift in your leadership if you allowed wholeness—not performance—to guide your next decision?

Complexity is not a threat to leadership — it is the place where wholeness begins.

CHAPTER 23

Living the Mosaic Way — Reflections in Real Life

Experience real-world stories of leaders who embody Mosaic Intelligence™ in action—across classrooms, boardrooms, communities, and cultures.

These are not case studies. They are windows into leadership that honors emotional integrity, cultural flexibility, and identity agility. Each person featured here chose to lead from wholeness in a world that often rewards fragmentation. Their stories offer not just inspiration—but possibility.

Vignette 1: Leading at the Edge of Respectability

Context: Corporate Leadership

Dionne, the newly appointed Vice President of Culture and People at a Fortune 500 company, is the only Black woman on the executive team. The company praises innovation but quietly maintains the status quo. During a leadership retreat, a senior colleague jokes, "We brought you in to shake things up—but don't shake too hard."

She laughs politely, but her body tightens. She knows this moment. She's been here before—celebrated in public, constrained in private.

Later in the meeting, when strategic goals are reviewed, Dionne speaks.

"We cannot discuss future readiness if we continue to avoid present discomfort. Our people are exhausted. The culture needs repair—not perks."

The room goes still. No one interrupts.

Dionne doesn't shout. She speaks plainly, with conviction. Her tone is calibrated, her presence grounded. She balances the weight of truth with the awareness of power dynamics. This is not performance. It's presence.

Her Mosaic Intelligence Method™ in action:

Emotional Integrity: Voicing truth with calm clarity
Cultural Flexibility: Speaking a difficult truth in a language the room could receive
Identity Agility: Remaining whole in a space that often rewards fragmentation

The opportunity:

To challenge the myth that influence requires assimilation. Dionne expands the room by standing fully in her truth. She invites others to redefine what leadership sounds and feels like.

What if the real work of innovation begins with emotional honesty?

Vignette 2: Teaching Across Borders

Context: Cross-Cultural Education

Logan arrives at an international school in the Middle East with lesson plans designed to spark conversation. But in his classroom, students remain silent, deferential. Eye contact is avoided. Participation is cautious.

At first, he interprets the silence as resistance. Then, he starts to listen—not to respond, but to learn.

A local colleague helps him see: silence here is not disengagement, but reverence. Reflection is valued over reaction. Expression is often nonverbal.

Logan begins to shift. He offers multiple modes of participation. He listens more. He lets go of the need to be the expert.

His Mosaic Intelligence Method™ in action:

Emotional Integrity: Letting go of control to embrace understanding
Cultural Flexibility: Reframing silence as emotional expression
Identity Agility: Moving from teacher to learner without losing leadership

The opportunity:

To make space for unfamiliar forms of brilliance. Logan doesn't abandon his values—he expands his view of learning.
What if your leadership could adapt without diminishing your core?

Vignette 3: Resisting Reduction

Context: Institutional Leadership in Resistant Systems

Angelica is a queer Afro-Latina leader in a federal agency. She is both strategist and culture bearer. In meeting after meeting, her proposals are softened or sidelined. Her insights are welcomed, but only when made palatable.

After yet another diluted strategy session, she decides to shift. That evening, she writes a memo.

"We cannot expect public trust if we reproduce silence within our own leadership culture. Equity is not branding. It is behavior."

She sends it to leadership. The next day, the air in the room shifts. No one says much. But something has landed.

Her Mosaic Intelligence Method™ in action:

Emotional Integrity: Naming what others avoid without self-erasure
Cultural Flexibility: Matching tone to audience without muting truth
Identity Agility: Refusing to perform comfort for institutional survival

The opportunity:

To move equity from concept to practice. Angelica doesn't ask for permission. She models emotional clarity as a leadership standard.
What if disrupting comfort is a sacred responsibility?

Vignette 4: Generations in the Mirror

Context: Family Business and Emotional Legacy

Malik, a Millennial, manages the family business founded by his father, a Baby Boomer who built the company through grit, sacrifice, and perseverance. Although the business has thrived for decades, its internal culture reflects a bygone era—emotionally rigid, prioritizing silence over vulnerability, and emphasizing work over wellness.

When Malik proposes a mental health policy for the staff, his father frowns.

"We didn't need all that. We just focused on our work. This is how businesses operate."

Instead of arguing, Malik listens—not only to his father's words, but to the generational pain underneath them. Later that evening, he writes a letter—not to confront, but to honor.

"Your survival built this. My healing will sustain it. We are not replacing legacy; we are expanding it."

A few days later, his father returns the letter with a handwritten note: "Thank you for seeing me."

Malik didn't just introduce a policy; he initiated a generational repair.

His Mosaic Intelligence Method™ in action:

Emotional Integrity: Honoring truth without shaming the past
Cultural Flexibility: Speaking across generational gaps with care
Identity Agility: Integrating healing into the fabric of inherited leadership

The opportunity:

To transition leadership from legacy preservation to legacy evolution. Malik doesn't discard what came before him; he enhances it with emotional nuance and clarity. His willingness to pause, honor the past, and lead with honesty provides his team—and his family—with a new way forward. In doing so, he connects survival and sustainability. The business transforms from a mere livelihood into a space where emotional growth is not just accepted but ingrained in its future.

What if evolving a legacy requires more courage than preserving it?

Vignette 5: The Courage to Recalibrate

Context: Bridge-Building Across Racial Differences

Emily, a senior leader at a nonprofit centered on equity and inclusion, is widely respected for her advocacy. She has led DEI trainings, coached diverse teams, and invested in personal growth. She prides herself on being deeply aware—until a quiet moment calls her further.

During a strategy meeting, she unintentionally interrupts her Black colleague—twice. He does not react during the meeting, but circles back later with grace and directness.

"I know it wasn't intentional, but it's happened before. I just needed you to know how it landed."

Emily's stomach drops. Her first instinct is to defend, explain, assure. But she stops herself.

"Thank you for trusting me with that. I want to get better—not just be seen as someone who 'gets it.'"

Later that week, she raises the incident during a team check-in—not to perform guilt, but to model accountability.

"This work isn't about appearances. It's about presence. And sometimes, that means naming our impact even when our intent was clean."

Her Mosaic Intelligence Method™ in action:

Emotional Integrity: Enduring discomfort without collapsing into guilt
Cultural Flexibility: Adjusting her leadership tone to foster emotional safety
Identity Agility: Letting go of the need to be perceived as "good" in order to grow

The opportunity:

To move allyship from theory to emotional practice. Emily models what it looks like to stay in the room emotionally, even when challenged. Her humility becomes a quiet revolution—making it safe for others to speak truth without fear of retribution.

What if true allyship begins not with answers, but with emotional presence?

Vignette 6: The Invisible Undercurrent

Context: Navigating Perceived Sabotage in the Workplace

Sasha, a high-performing project manager at a competitive tech firm, has earned promotion after promotion. But with each step upward, resistance grows louder—though never directly. She's excluded from meetings, given vague feedback, and once, a critical document disappears hours before a key presentation.

Her instincts say it's sabotage. But without proof, she knows she must choose her next steps wisely.

She tightens systems. Documents everything. Clarifies communications in writing. But more than tactics, she turns inward. She examines her own fear—not as weakness, but as data. In therapy and quiet reflection, she explores what this tension is teaching her.

Then, she initiates calm, direct conversations with key colleagues—naming issues without blame. Her tone shifts from defensiveness to self-possession. A new layer of clarity emerges. She becomes less reactive, more rooted.

Her Mosaic Intelligence Method™ in action:

Emotional Integrity: Naming internal fear without letting it rule her response

Cultural Flexibility: Navigating a competitive culture without mirroring its toxicity

Identity Agility: Holding on to her self-worth without needing constant validation

The opportunity:

To meet sabotage with structure, and power plays with presence. Sasha's approach reminds us that resilience is not retaliation—it is emotional clarity in motion.

What if clarity is your most potent form of resistance?

Vignette 7: "I Just Don't Like Them"

Context: When Your Spirit Rejects Someone—And You're Not Sure Why

Amira, a department chair known for emotional insight, finds herself irrationally irritated by a new colleague, Jordan. No major incident occurred—but something about Jordan's confidence triggers her.

Rather than dismiss Jordan or trust her bias, she turns inward.

"Why am I resistant to them? What part of me feels unseen or threatened?"

She realizes Jordan reminds her of a younger version of herself—a self once punished for boldness. This discomfort isn't about Jordan. It's about an old wound.

Instead of forcing connection, she softens. Stops overcorrecting. Makes room.

Her Mosaic Intelligence Method™ in action:

Emotional Integrity: Naming discomfort without projecting it
Cultural Flexibility: Questioning her own internalized beliefs about likability
Identity Agility: Reclaiming a silenced part of herself through another's mirror

The opportunity:

To turn irritation into insight. Amira learns that resistance is often a clue—an invitation to heal, not to judge.

What if the person you struggle with is revealing a part of you still waiting to be loved?

Vignette 8: The New Blueprint

Context: When the Old Model of Leadership No Longer Fits

Elliot, a seasoned executive, listens to yet another keynote on "resilient leadership"—toughness, decisiveness, unwavering confidence. The message lands hollow. Not because it's wrong, but because it's incomplete.

He has led through mergers, crises, and expansion. But the real challenges were never in the spreadsheets—they were in the culture. Burnout masked as commitment. Disconnection mistaken for efficiency.

After the session, he turns to his Chief People Officer.

"What if we stop rewarding emotional detachment? What if we became a Mosaic Organization?"

Together, they redesign leadership training. They talk less about grit and more about grounding. They build emotional fluency into management expectations. They revise policies to center lived experience—not just productivity.

Their Mosaic Intelligence Method™ in action:

Emotional Integrity: Admitting what no longer works
Cultural Flexibility: Building systems around real people, not idealized roles
Identity Agility: Allowing leadership to evolve alongside the world

The opportunity:

To reimagine leadership as wholeness in action. Elliot shows us that systems change doesn't require a revolution—it begins with one honest conversation and the courage to act on it.

What if the future of leadership is already here—just waiting to be named?

LIVING THE MOSAIC WAY

Mosaic Intelligence is not about mastering a framework—it's about living a truth. These prompts help you pause and assess how you're embodying the path of wholeness.

- Which pillar do you most naturally embody—and which one invites you to stretch?
- How might you begin weaving all three into your leadership, parenting, or presence this week?
- What would it look like to lead from wholeness instead of from habit?

Wholeness is not a privilege. It is the quiet revolution we need in every room.

CHAPTER 24

The Mosaic Method's Limits — Practicing With Integrity

E xamine the ethical edges of this work, acknowledging the emotional labor, systemic challenges, and shared responsibility required to lead from wholeness.

This is your invitation to lead with emotional integrity, cultural flexibility, and identity agility in a world that needs all three.

Whether you are a leader, coach, educator, or changemaker, the Mosaic Intelligence Method™ offers you not just a framework—but a pathway. But even the most visionary frameworks require discernment. Before we move into the next chapter of impact, we must first name the limitations with integrity.

The Limits of the Mosaic Intelligence Method™

Every transformative method must carry with it a word of caution—a recognition that no single tool, no matter how powerful, is a cure-all. The Mosaic Intelligence Method™ is not a shortcut to change, but a compass toward wholeness. It is both profound and partial. Empowering and imperfect. And acknowledging its boundaries is not a contradiction of its worth—it is a deepening of its wisdom.

1. **It Is Not a Shortcut to Justice**

Emotional literacy is not a replacement for structural change. The Mosaic Intelligence Method™ cannot substitute for policy reform, economic justice, or systemic accountability. It does not dismantle oppression on its own.

But it can deepen our capacity to lead that work with truth, humility, and integrity. Emotional clarity must walk alongside structural clarity. Wholeness is powerful—but it cannot act alone.

2. **It Requires Emotional Labor—Often Without External Validation**

Mosaic leaders model alignment rather than performance, presence rather than perfection. In environments that reward speed, certainty, and output, that work can go unseen—or even dismissed.

This method often asks more of those already carrying the most: women, Black and Brown leaders, LGBTQIA+ professionals, and individuals navigating intersecting identities. Without communal honor and shared responsibility, it becomes an invisible tax. When emotional safety is absent, wholeness turns from a balm into a burden.

3. **It May Be Dismissed as Soft or Idealistic**

The Mosaic Intelligence Method™ centers emotion, identity, nuance, and complexity—all qualities that can be misunderstood in systems rooted in linear thinking and efficiency. Without proper framing, it risks being reduced to inspirational language or misused as emotional performance.

To maintain its power, it must be taught, practiced, and modeled with care. It must remain accountable to both research and reality.

4. **It Is Not Quick, Linear, or Easily Replicable**

This is not a five-step formula. There is no neat resolution to becoming more whole. Some days, wholeness will feel elusive. Some seasons will feel like regression. Healing is not a straight line. Culture change is not a checklist.

The Mosaic Intelligence Method™ is an ongoing practice—one that requires time, tension, and courageous iteration.

5. **It Requires Collective Practice—Not Individual Mastery**

No single leader can carry the emotional weight of an entire culture. No one should have to. This framework is designed to live in community, not isolation. Wholeness is not just a personal responsibility—it is a cultural ethic.

When organizations expect individuals to "be the bridge" without support, they reinforce the very harm they seek to heal. Shared emotional responsibility is not optional—it is essential.

Why These Limits Matter

Naming these limitations does not dilute the Mosaic Intelligence Method™. It matures it. It protects its essence from misuse and allows us to engage it honestly.

True leadership does not require perfection—it requires integrity. This work is not about being flawless. It is about being faithful. It is about showing up, again and again, with open eyes and an anchored heart.

Bringing Mosaic Into the World

The Mosaic Intelligence Method™ is more than a concept. It is a lens. A language. A way of leading and being that centers emotional fluency in an emotionally fragmented world.

If you feel called to bring this work into your organization, classroom, community, or practice, you are not alone. Whether you pursue facilitator certification, a leadership retreat, or simply a conversation that begins with presence, your impact matters.

Visit mosaicintelligencemethod.com to explore next steps. The toolkit, training, and community await.

Throughout this book, we have explored what it means to feel deeply, connect truthfully, and lead with presence. We've walked through resilience, identity, disruption, healing, parenting, and possibility. The Mosaic Intelligence Method™ brings these threads together—and offers us a path forward.

You are not just implementing a framework.

You are helping restore wholeness.

One decision. One conversation. One presence at a time.

Reflection

PRACTICING WITH INTEGRITY

- Where in your leadership or life might you be carrying too much alone?
- What systems around you need to evolve in order to support emotional wholeness?
- How can you honor this method without overextending yourself?

The Mosaic Intelligence Method™ will never be a miracle. But it will always be a mirror—one that reflects who you are and who you are becoming.

CONCLUSION

The Way Forward — Building a More Emotionally Connected World

As we move beyond the final chapter, one truth remains: the world is not waiting for the most knowledgeable leader—it is longing for the most grounded one.

This book has invited you to reimagine leadership—not as a title to hold, but as a way of being rooted in presence and relationship. Together, we've explored the many forms of disruption—from global shifts to personal doubt—and uncovered the emotional tools that allow us to meet uncertainty with integrity, not fear. We've redefined empathy as strategy, not sentiment. And we've dismantled the belief that clarity depends on certainty—showing instead that emotional depth can illuminate the path, even when the destination is unknown.

We are entering a leadership era where adaptability is not just about change management—it is about emotional agility. Where innovation is not simply measured by what we create, but by the cultures we shape. Where wholeness is no longer optional, but a defining necessity for transformative leadership.

The Mosaic Intelligence Method™ offers a new compass. It is not a framework for perfection—it is a pathway to presence. It invites us to lead with emotional literacy, cultural wisdom, and identity evolution at the core.

Emotional Literacy teaches us to name what we feel so we can own what we say and do.

Cultural Flexibility equips us to navigate complexity with grace, honoring difference while staying grounded in self.

Identity Agility gives us the freedom to evolve our leadership without losing our center.

This is the language of the future. It's what will differentiate those who manage from those who transform.

And yet, The Mosaic Way is not a strategy you apply—it is a path you walk. A way of being you embody.

Living the Mosaic Way: What It Means to Lead With Wholeness

To live as a Mosaic leader is to reject the idea that emotional fragmentation is the cost of success. It is to build systems without abandoning soul. It is to choose presence over performance and connection over control.

Mosaic leadership means:

- Creating emotionally attuned workplaces—not just productive ones.
- Building relationships that honor cultural nuance—not just shared goals.
- Allowing your identity to stretch without fear that it's breaking.
- Choosing to lead from what is most human—not what is most strategic.

Your impact will not be measured by how well you replicate old models, but by how deeply you reflect your values in motion.

Wholeness is not the end of your leadership journey—it is the beginning of your legacy.

Let this be your invitation:

Start with awareness.
Deepen through curiosity.
Sustain through integrity.

You don't need to lead perfectly. You need to lead from truth.
That truth lives in your Mosaic.
And The Mosaic Way is how you walk it.

EPILOGUE

Wholeness Is the Way Forward

This is more than the end of a book—it is the beginning of a new way of seeing ourselves, each other, and the world we are called to lead.

Throughout these pages, we have walked through turbulence and stillness, crisis and clarity, fragmentation and restoration. We have named our feelings, confronted our blind spots, and reimagined leadership—not as control or charisma, but as care. What we have explored is not simply emotional intelligence; it is the deeper language of wholeness.

The Mosaic Intelligence Method™ was born out of this very tension—a recognition that traditional emotional intelligence must now expand into a more inclusive capacity: one of emotional literacy, cultural fluency, and identity integration. It must evolve as we evolve.

The Mosaic Way asks us to lead with:

Emotional Literacy, because language gives shape to healing.

Cultural Flexibility, because leadership must transcend borders.

Identity Agility, because who we are is never static—and neither is our influence.

These are not skills to be mastered. They are ways of being to be embodied.

To walk The Mosaic Way is to live with your pieces visible and your story intact. It is to lead from your humanity—not in spite of it, but because of it.

So no, this is not a return to what was. It is a quiet, steady revolution.

It is a restoration. A reckoning. A remembering.

It is the call to be whole—and to lead from that wholeness.

This is The Mosaic Way.

Walk it with courage.

Live it with clarity.

Lead it with love.

Always.

GLOSSARY OF KEY TERMS

The Mosaic Intelligence Method™ builds upon the foundation of emotional intelligence, expanding it into a multidimensional framework rooted in emotional integrity, cultural flexibility, and identity agility. It introduces three core leadership capacities essential for twenty-first-century wholeness in an age of fragmentation: emotional literacy, cultural fluency, and identity integration—applied expressions of its foundational pillars.

Accountability
The willingness to take ownership of one's actions, behaviors, and impact without deflecting blame. In emotionally aligned leadership, accountability fosters trust and repair.

Attunement
The capacity to sense, interpret, and respond to the emotional cues of others. It reflects deep listening and connection beyond words.

Authenticity
The congruence between one's inner values and outward behavior. Authentic leaders express themselves with emotional honesty and integrity.

Belonging
A felt sense of acceptance and emotional safety without needing to assimilate or alter one's identity. It is a core human need in all relational spaces.

Boundary
An intentional limit that protects emotional, mental, or physical well-being. Emotionally attuned boundaries are set with both compassion and clarity, honoring both self-respect and relational integrity.

Clarity
The state of being emotionally and mentally lucid. Clarity helps leaders make decisions rooted in alignment, not reactivity.

Compassion Fatigue
The emotional depletion that can result from prolonged caregiving or emotional labor. It signals the need for restoration and support.

Co-Regulation
A relational process where two or more individuals help stabilize one another's emotional states through presence, tone, and responsiveness.

Cultural Attunement
The sensitivity and skill to respond to cultural differences with humility, curiosity, and emotional presence.

Cultural Flexibility
The capacity to engage across cultural, generational, and social differences without losing your sense of self. It involves empathy, curiosity, and adaptability in diverse contexts. A core pillar of the Mosaic Intelligence Method™.

Curiosity
An emotionally attuned practice grounded in inquiry, openness, and the suspension of judgment—especially in unfamiliar, tense, or complex situations. Curiosity invites connection, deepens understanding, and fosters psychological safety.

Emotional Adaptability
The ability to remain emotionally effective amid change, complexity, or ambiguity. It supports resilience and openness.

Emotional Agility
The skill of staying emotionally present and flexible, especially during discomfort. It involves acknowledging emotions without being hijacked by them.

Emotional Alignment
The integration of emotional insight, inner values, and external actions. It is foundational to trust-building and sustainable leadership.

Emotional Attunement
The capacity to be emotionally in sync with others—reading cues, responding with sensitivity, and holding space without imposing control. It reflects both presence and humility, especially in multicultural or relationally complex settings.

Emotional Availability
The capacity to be emotionally present, responsive, and engaged with others. It nurtures connection and relational trust.

Emotional Capacity
The energy, bandwidth, and inner space needed to process emotions, hold space for others, and respond without overwhelm.

Emotional Clarity
The accurate recognition and articulation of emotional states. It supports wise decision-making and relational authenticity.

Emotional Depth
A grounded and mature emotional awareness that extends beyond momentary reactions. Emotional depth allows individuals to hold complexity, remain present in discomfort, and draw from a well of reflection and insight.

Emotional Design
The intentional shaping of environments to foster emotional safety, connection, and belonging—physically, relationally, or digitally.

Emotional Discernment
The capacity to interpret and understand emotions with nuance, allowing for informed and compassionate responses.

Emotional Fluency *(evolved from Emotional Intelligence)*
Emotional fluency expands upon the foundation of emotional intelligence. It is the capacity to recognize, regulate, and respond to one's own emotions—and those of others—with presence, clarity, and care. It emphasizes relational nuance and internal integrity over performative control. Emotional fluency supports personal growth, relational depth, and culturally responsive leadership by enabling individuals to name, navigate, and express emotions with intentionality.

Note: Previously referred to as emotional intelligence, this evolved term reflects a broader, more integrated capacity for emotional and relational awareness.

Emotional Honesty
The ability to name one's emotions truthfully and without performance. It supports vulnerability, integrity, and connection.

Emotional Integrity
The alignment between what you feel, what you value, and how you show up. It is the foundation of trust and authenticity in emotionally intelligent leadership. It is the first pillar of the Mosaic Intelligence Method™ and a foundation for trust.

Emotional Labor
The invisible effort of managing emotional expression to meet social or professional expectations, often at the cost of personal authenticity.

Emotional Legacy
The emotional patterns, behaviors, and beliefs inherited across generations. Emotionally fluent individuals examine and evolve these legacies.

Emotional Literacy
The skill of identifying, expressing, and understanding emotional experiences with nuance and precision.

Emotional Maturity
The ability to navigate emotional complexity with grace, empathy, and accountability. It includes taking ownership of one's emotional impact.

Emotional Presence
The quality of being fully emotionally engaged in the moment, attuned to both oneself and others. Presence communicates care without words.

Emotional Resonance
The capacity to create an emotional impact through authentic alignment between feeling and expression. Resonance fosters trust, connection, and collective energy.

Emotional Wholeness
A state of emotional integration where past wounds, present awareness, and future vision coexist in harmony. It reflects healing and the ability to lead from a grounded, compassionate place.

Empathy
The skill of emotionally connecting with and understanding another person's experience, even when it differs from your own.

Grounded Awareness
A centered state of being that fosters calm, intentional, and emotionally attuned responses. It is the foundation of emotional regulation, clarity, and aligned leadership—especially in moments of uncertainty or stress.

Identity Agility
The ability to lead from a dynamic and evolving sense of self. Leaders with identity agility embrace change, hold multiple truths, and guide

others with grounded fluidity. A core pillar of the Mosaic Intelligence Method™.

Identity Dissonance
The tension that arises when your environment or expectations conflict with your sense of self. It often emerges during transitions or cultural shifts.

Inclusive Leadership
A relational style of leadership grounded in emotional integrity, cultural humility, and identity awareness. It centers wholeness, psychological safety, and shared humanity.

Inner Clarity
A grounded understanding of one's internal emotional and mental landscape, enabling intentional leadership and alignment.

Inner Work
The personal practice of emotional reflection, healing, and growth that strengthens leadership and resilience.

Micro-Betrayal
Small, often unintentional acts that erode emotional safety—such as dismissing feelings, ignoring contributions, or avoiding accountability.

Mosaic Intelligence Method™
A three-pillar leadership framework that expands emotional intelligence to meet the needs of a fragmented, multicultural, and fast-changing world. It integrates emotional integrity, cultural flexibility, and identity agility to foster inclusive, values-driven leadership.

Narrative Identity
The evolving story we tell ourselves about who we are, shaped by culture, values, memory, and experience.

Psychological Safety
The belief that a space allows for honesty, vulnerability, and risk without fear of punishment or humiliation.

Regulation
The ability to skillfully manage one's emotional responses, particularly in challenging situations. It supports connection and calm.

Relational Intelligence
The ability to navigate interpersonal dynamics with awareness, empathy, and emotional clarity.

Repair
The process of restoring emotional trust after rupture through acknowledgment, accountability, and reconnection.

Self-Awareness
The capacity to recognize and understand your own emotional states, motivations, and behaviors. It is the root of all emotional growth.

Self-Leadership
The ability to guide, regulate, and align oneself emotionally, especially in the absence of external direction.

Social Intelligence
The skill of navigating interpersonal relationships, reading emotional cues, and building trust in diverse social settings.

Trauma-Informed
An approach rooted in understanding the emotional impact of trauma. It emphasizes safety, empathy, and empowerment.

Wholeness
A state of integrated identity where one leads, lives, and relates from emotional alignment—not fragmentation.

DISCUSSION GUIDE

Reflect. Relate. Reimagine.

This guide is designed to help you engage more deeply with the core themes in *The Mosaic Way*. Whether you are reading this book individually, with a team, or as part of a learning community, these prompts will invite you to reflect inwardly, relate the content to your lived experience, and reimagine how you lead, live, and connect in a rapidly changing world.

You can use these questions as journaling prompts, group discussion starters, or personal coaching reflections. Come back to them often. The goal is not to arrive at perfect answers—but to cultivate presence, integrity, and emotional fluency as you evolve.

Section I: The Emotional Landscape of Our Time

Reflect:
What emotion have you most often ignored or numbed? Why?

Relate:
How has prolonged disruption shaped how you show up—at work, at home, or within yourself?

Reimagine:
What would it look like to lead with emotional presence in a world that rewards performance?

Section II: Leading with Emotional Integrity

Reflect:
When have you chosen control over connection? What did it cost you?

Relate:
How do your behaviors create—or restrict—psychological safety for others across lines of difference?

Reimagine:
What's one way you could lead with more empathy, humility, or emotional courage this week?

Section III: Emotional Intelligence for Healing and Justice

Reflect:
What belief or system have you internalized that no longer aligns with your values?

Relate:
Where have you silenced yourself to belong—and what did it teach you about power or protection?

Reimagine:
What would it mean to lead justly, even if it disrupts comfort or tradition?

Section IV: Designing the Future with EQ

Reflect:
What digital habit has influenced how you connect—or disconnect—from others?

Relate:
How does your environment support—or sabotage—emotional wellness, especially across identities?

Reimagine:
What kind of emotionally intelligent and inclusive space do you want to create?

Section V: Identity, Belonging, and Global Leadership

Reflect:
What part of your identity do you wish others would see more clearly?

Relate:
When have you been the outsider? How did you adapt—and how did it shape your leadership?

Reimagine:
What does it look like to lead with both rooted identity and cultural agility?

Section VI: Living the Mosaic Way

Reflect:
Which pillar—emotional integrity, cultural flexibility, or identity agility—feels most natural to you? Which one stretches you the most?

Relate:
How have these pillars helped you lead through uncertainty, complexity, or change?

Reimagine:
What commitment can you make today to lead with wholeness and inclusion—even in a fragmented world?

To better echo the themes of evolution and inclusion, you might consider this slight tweak:

This guide was never meant to offer every answer.

It was written to remind you of who you are when you pause, reflect, listen, and lead with care.

Let it walk with you—one intentional moment at a time.

You are not simply enduring change; you are evolving within it.

And you are not leading alone—you are shaping a more inclusive world with every courageous step.

FURTHER READING & REFERENCES

The following sources have informed the research, insights, and practical frameworks woven throughout this book. While the writing is reflective and narrative in style, these works offer deeper context, validation, and extension for readers interested in the foundations of emotional intelligence, leadership, and cultural fluency.

Works by the Author

Thomas, K. (2010). *Uncertainty to Confidence: A New Way of Living Your Life.* New You Publishing.

A reflective guide to navigating life's uncertainties with emotional clarity, purpose, and resilience.

Thomas, K. (2012). *The Foolproof Woman's Guide to Strength, Strategy, and Self-Love in Relationships.* New You Publishing.

A self-help book offering insight and encouragement for women navigating love, personal boundaries, and emotional self-worth.

Thomas, K. (2020). *Identity of Western Teachers in the United Arab Emirates: A Qualitative Study.* Doctoral dissertation, American College of Education. ProQuest Dissertations Publishing.

Research exploring identity dissonance, belonging, and the social integration of Western educators in Eastern contexts.

Thomas, K., & Thomas, A. (2022). Case study on the adaptable social identity of expatriates and the effect of the local culture of Saudi Arabia. *Journal of Positive School Psychology, 6*(2), 109–114.

Qualitative research examining cultural identity adaptation and cross-cultural dynamics in the Gulf region.

Thomas, K. (2023). *Communication Skills for Insurance Adjusters: Maximizing Your Value to Insurance Companies While Prioritizing Self-Care.* Efficient Adjuster Publishing.

A practical guide for adjusters seeking to improve field communication while protecting their own well-being.

Thomas, K. (2025). *Communicate Connect and Lead.* Efficient Adjuster Publishing.

An expanded edition featuring updated case studies, reflection prompts, and strategies for emotionally attuned claims communication and leadership.

Thomas, K. (2025). *Claim the Lead: Coaching Over Control in the Claims Industry.* Efficient Adjuster Press.

A leadership guide redefining management culture in high-pressure claims environments through coaching, emotional intelligence, and sustainable performance.

Emotional Intelligence & Leadership

Goleman, D. (1995). *Emotional Intelligence: Why It Can Matter More Than IQ.* Bantam Books.
Bradberry, T., & Greaves, J. (2009). *Emotional Intelligence 2.0.* TalentSmart.
Harvard Business Review. (2017). *HBR's 10 Must Reads on Emotional Intelligence.* Harvard Business Review Press.

Education, Identity & Emotional Development

Collaborative for Academic, Social, and Emotional Learning (CASEL). *Core SEL Competencies.*
Center on the Developing Child at Harvard University. *Key Concepts in Brain Architecture and Executive Function.*
Yale Center for Emotional Intelligence.

Cultural Intelligence, Belonging & Global Identity

Livermore, D. (2015). *Leading with Cultural Intelligence.* AMACOM.
Hofstede, G. (2010). *Cultures and Organizations: Software of the Mind.* McGraw-Hill.
Tatum, B. D. (1997). *Why Are All the Black Kids Sitting Together in the Cafeteria?* Basic Books.

Workplace Well-Being & Psychological Safety

Gallup. (2023). *State of the Global Workplace Report.*
Google. *Project Aristotle: Re: Work Guide.*
Edmondson, A. C. (2018). *The Fearless Organization.* Wiley.

Generational Leadership & Systems Change

David, S. (2016). *Emotional Agility: Get Unstuck, Embrace Change, and Thrive.* Avery.
Brown, B. (2018). *Dare to Lead.* Random House.
Kegan, R., & Lahey, L. L. (2009). *Immunity to Change.* Harvard Business Press.

This book also draws upon the author's doctoral research, cross-cultural teaching experiences, and qualitative insights from Mosaic Intelligence Method™ workshops, coaching sessions, and leadership labs across diverse industries and global contexts.

CLOSING NOTE FROM THE AUTHOR

You made it through this book—which means you're already transforming the culture around you.

That's not a small thing. In a fast-moving world that demands performance over presence, you paused long enough to reflect, engage, and grow. That means you're already walking The Mosaic Way—a different kind of leadership rooted in emotional courage, cultural wisdom, and identity truth.

You might not feel ready. You may still feel fragmented or uncertain. But transformation doesn't begin when everything is figured out. It begins the moment we say yes to wholeness—especially when it's messy, unfinished, or in progress.

Maybe you picked up this book out of curiosity. Maybe it was exhaustion. Maybe something in your spirit whispered, "There has to be more than this." And maybe, as you read, you discovered you weren't alone—that what you've been sensing about leadership, culture, and yourself is not only valid, but shared and worthy of language.

You now have that language.

Whether you are leading a team, raising a child, teaching a class, or simply navigating the messiness of your own evolution, you are not starting from scratch. You are building with wisdom. You are creating with intention. You are showing up not as a perfected self, but as a present one.

That is The Mosaic Way™.

That is the Mosaic Intelligence Method™ in motion.

As you close this book, I hope you also open something deeper within yourself—a sacred permission to lead with integrity, complexity, and heart. You don't need to have all the answers. You just need to be fully present.

The world doesn't need louder voices.

It needs truer ones.

And yours—just as it is—is enough.

With gratitude and deep belief in your journey,

— *Dr. Karissa Thomas*

ACKNOWLEDGMENTS

This book embodies years of personal reflection, professional insight, cultural exploration, and sacred dialogue. It was conceived in boardrooms and classrooms, across continents and cultures, during quiet journaling moments and courageous conversations. The Mosaic Intelligence Method™ could not have come to life without the stories, struggles, and wisdom of those who dared to lead with heart—even when the world urged them to fragment.

To the mentors, colleagues, and students who invited me to see beyond conventional models of leadership—thank you for your honesty, your challenges, and your vision. You helped shape the framework now woven into these pages.

To my family and friends, thank you for holding space for both my vulnerability and my strength—for reminding me that wholeness is not a destination, but a way of being.

To the global community that shaped this work—from Dubai to Manhattan, Uganda to Mumbai—your voices, silences, and emotional truths taught me what no textbook ever could. You revealed the living power of culture, identity, and emotional integrity in real time.

And to every leader, learner, and truth-teller who has shared their stories of rupture and repair—this book would not exist without you. Your courage to feel, your willingness to unlearn, and your quiet commitment to becoming whole have been the heartbeat of this journey.

This work is dedicated to those who are creating emotionally attuned spaces—not from perfection, but from presence.

May we continue to lead with care, live with clarity, and connect with intention.

ABOUT THE AUTHOR

Dr. Karissa Thomas is a global leadership strategist, international speaker, and award-winning author of *Uncertainty to Confidence: A New Way of Living Your Life*. She is best known for pioneering the **Mosaic Intelligence Method**™—a transformative framework that redefines emotional leadership through fluency, presence, and culturally responsive wisdom. Her work addresses the urgent challenges of leading during times of disruption, cultural complexity, and global change.

With over two decades of experience in corporate leadership, cross-cultural education, and international consulting, Dr. Thomas has led transformational initiatives across the United States, the Middle East, and beyond. She holds a Doctorate in Educational Leadership and an Executive MBA, allowing her to bridge rigorous research with real-world leadership demands.

As the creator of the Mosaic Intelligence Method™, she empowers individuals and organizations to lead with emotional wholeness, cultural wisdom, and identity integrity across lines of difference. Her work centers on building emotionally attuned ecosystems—where self-awareness, accountability, and connection are not just aspirational values, but measurable, lived outcomes.

Bring This Work to Life in Your Community

Become a Certified Mosaic Intelligence Method™ Facilitator

If this book resonated with you, imagine the impact of guiding others through its insights—facilitating conversations that heal, connect, and empower across teams, classrooms, communities, and leadership spaces.

The **Mosaic Intelligence Method™ Facilitator Certification** equips you to lead experiences grounded in:

Emotional Integrity — modeling presence, reflection, and internal leadership

Cultural Flexibility — navigating difference with humility and wisdom

Identity Agility — helping others evolve without losing who they are

As a certified facilitator, you will receive:

- A comprehensive facilitator toolkit with scripts, activities, and reflection cards
- Access to exclusive training and ongoing support
- Licensing to use the Mosaic Intelligence Method™ in your professional setting
- Connection to a global community of emotionally attuned practitioners

Whether you are a coach, consultant, educator, or organizational leader, this method empowers you to lead with wholeness and foster spaces of psychological safety and transformation.

Step into the next level of impact.
Learn more: www.mosaicintelligencemethod.com
Inquire: info@mosaicintelligencemethod.com

www.ingramcontent.com/pod-product-compliance
Lightning Source LLC
Chambersburg PA
CBHW051939290426
44110CB00015B/2041